The Heart of Life

a Soul-full guide for relating on planet Earth

in dedication to every Soul with whom I have ever, or ever shall,

share love and deep affection ...

David Charles Rowan

The Heart of Life

a Soul-full guide for relating on planet Earth

Contents:

Introduction - a relationship with relating

We humans are relational creatures. Whether we enjoy the company of others or prefer being in our own space, we are enacting a particular orientation to the dynamic of being one of more than seven billion souls currently incarnated in human form on planet Earth.

Spiritual and Esoteric philosophies have a number of different viewpoints and schools of thought about the nature of being human and our relationship with a broader or higher form of consciousness; often described as a God or a Goddess or a pantheon of Gods and Goddesses, or, more simply as a relationship with The Light or The Universe. These perspectives may be described as a sense of consciousness relating with the sky. Humanistic philosophies describe a relationship with one's own innate being and the world we find ourselves in; Buddhism, Psychology and life sciences are examples of this Earthy lens of reality. I use the term, 'lens of reality', with deliberate intent. The 7 billion + humans currently on earth each have their own unique subjective perspective of reality and life and the sense of self that experiences life.

The human condition holds such a diverse rainbow of viewpoints, positions and perspectives that to write on the topic of relating through every possible hue would not only be a task of Herculean proportions, it would far exceed the possibilities of this pocket book. Given the restrictions imposed by such a confined space, I am only able to write from my own subjective perspective; in short, this is a Rowan's eye view of human relating. In social media profiles I describe myself as: 'Pagan, with Zen-like leanings'. Initiated into Witchcraft in British Craft tradition, a teacher of Astrology and Esoteric Studies for 25 years, a student of lay Psychology and a teacher of Neuro-Holistic Therapy (Psychobiology, Hypnotherapy and NLP) for 23 years, a holder of 2 masters degrees: an MA in Cultural Astronomy and Psychology and an MSc in Psycho-Social Studies and currently taking a 3rd masters, an MSc in Psychology and 28 years of conducting and teaching Past Life Regression techniques have given me the opportunity to spend more than a quarter of a century with students and clients exploring their personal intimate relationships and relationships with life in general.

The Heart of Life, this little book of love, has blossomed from these learning experiences and encounters with a wide variety of people over this lifetime. At times I may speak from the first person, giving my own subjective views and opinions and I trust my explorations into the nature of being human in this life have a breadth of insight and illumination worthy of value for you.

David Charles Rowan

November 2016

A Soul's Journey

The Soul purpose of incarnation and experiencing many lives

As above ...

From a soul-perspective, I see this world like a term in school, and the 'place' we reside in both before we enter this life, and to where we return afterwards is our true home.

To me, it seems that, if this is an infant school where we may learn about things like greed, sadism, avarice, malevolence etc, then great souls like Osiris, Jesus, Buddha, Pythagoras, Mohamed, Arthur, Confucius etc became the highest students of this school, like prefects of this world; a state of consciousness I can only but glimmer at this time, but to which I aspire.

Then, it follows that these 'prefect souls' would be in the first year of the next school - the juniors. I have no idea what a prefect of that school would be like because I can barely comprehend being a prefect of this one. And, as for the prefects of the highest university ...

My current comprehension of life here is a kind of muddling through the enormity of the possibilities of life, and of being me, and doing my best to help and assist others with love, kindness and compassion wherever possible.

The periods between lives, for me, are our school holidays, in which we consolidate what we have learned, play and catch up with friends and then begin to configure the next lessons.

Sleep/dreaming is the astral journey we all take home, after each day's class; meditation, trance, relaxation, are little trips home; like stepping out of the dream and waking for a moment ...

In a healthy body each cell asserts its individuality and purpose in harmony with the whole body.

In a healthy society each individual asserts their unique identity and purpose in accordance with the harmony of the whole collective society.

If we take it that a Soul is a cell in the body of spiritual light of what some term 'God', then our purpose is to assert our true and unique selves in harmony with the desires and wishes of all other life forms – including all other levels of spiritual existence.

This is a tall order – it's enough for people to be in harmony with the body they reside in, let alone all the other bodies around them as well.

If we are not in harmony with our bodies then sometimes a cell will assert its individual identity – not in accordance with the whole body. This cell is just 'out on its own', doing 'its own thing'. When it replicates itself, or spreads its influence, and there is a crowd of cells 'doing their own thing' without reference to the rest of the system, and without being brought into harmony by the immune system, we say the body has an unwanted, and 'out of control' growth; we may call this 'cancer'.

If you consider there are individuals in society that act without reference to the harmony of their collective fellow Earth sharers, and the upholders of laws of peaceful co-existence are unable to bring them into harmony, then we could say society, or the consciousness of mankind is also at dis-ease.

If we hold the view that all Souls are, 'children of the Light, and we, as 'cells in the body of God', fail to act in harmony with all beings of creation then we could say 'God is at dis-ease', and we are a-live in the process of the healing of God; the return to divine harmony via the harmonisation of each individual cell, or Soul , or fragment of universal light. Life in this physical world for us human beings is the state of being a Spirit while being sensual , at once we are both divine and mortal, conscious and unconscious; insignificant and very very special.

In being incarnated into physical matter we are like nerve endings in the body of 'God'. All that we do, think, feel and experience is automatically 'transmitted' into the realm of spirit and spread into the great collective spiritual web from which all life forms obtain their life force – some call this 'pranya' and some call this 'the collective unconscious'. The 'stuff' of our experiences is spread throughout the collective for any/and all life forms to pick up on – or, 'unconsciously download' into their personal unconscious – which their conscious mind (if they have one) may, or may not, be able to access & experience. The easiest image that comes to mind is a fairground 'dodgem car'. Each car, while being an individual, is connected to the great grid from which it receives its vital energy. This downloaded stuff may or may not be consciously acknowledged. From a human perspective this can have a powerful effect upon behaviour, and the consequential future.

The impulse drive within every form of life is towards improvement – evolution. Spiritually the impulse drive is towards perfect harmony – to become 'at-one' with light itself. This state has to be internally driven from the heart of our being, the cell – or Soul – has to naturally fall into the state of harmony. Each Soul is given complete free will so that it clearly chooses its pathway towards harmony, or dis-harmony; ease, or dis-ease. Spirituality is not born from dictatorship.

Upon reaching the state of harmony the collective is brightened by one more 'star' 'reaching the light', or one more 'cell in the body of God' returning to a state of health and purity and unity. One by one the harmony spreads and the healing becomes stronger; the body of light becomes brighter still and the energy spirals into more and more uplifting states of beauty, harmony and perfection.

As the Soul progresses towards harmony on every level of experience it will have deliberately and sustainably chosen to continue travelling in that direction. This means a Soul will encounter obstacles to harmony (reflecting its own inner dis-harmony) on every conceivable level of experience so that it is given the opportunity to:

Experience -Comprehend - Explore - Familiarise - Build know-ledges - Remember - Understand - Transform - Evolve - Harmonise - Master.

Mastery of every level of experience, of every kind of experience, is the remit of incarnation is this physical realm. It is very challenging, slow, and wonderfully fulfilling.

Humans are endowed with an innate capacity for learning ... to me, learning is not a gift - it is an activity, and various humans conduct this activity extensively or moderately; diplomacy, tact, musicianship, art, and all skills can be learned. For some, the learning comes swiftly because their innate nature already has prowess along that path, but that does not exclude a less endowed human from learning - it just means those humans have to muster a more concerted effort and degree of concentration; with infinite persistence and patience, we can all learn ... to me, that is the nature of human incarnation ...

We are Souls in Earth-School and we are teaching our hearts to default to an orientation of kindness, love and compassion through a 360-wide spectrum of experiences of these things and also their opposites, in order for our hearts to learn to choose the default position of wisdom; having and showing, sounds knowledge of judgement through one's reactions and behaviour.

'Who looks outside, dreams. Who looks inside, wakes'. C.G. Jung

Earth School

Self Discipline in terms of being a disciple of the Self

Free-Won't in contrast with Free-Will

In 2011, the Harvard professor of Psychology, Stephen Pinker, published a book on the decline of violence in human civilisations; *The Better Angels of Our Nature*. In this well researched and fascinating book, Pinker shows with repeated evidence that over long periods of time, societies are becoming increasingly intolerant of violence. If you are ever feeling pessimistic about society or culture and the general direction in which humans seem to be heading, I highly recommend The Better Angels of Our Nature for a solid platform of evidence for having a real and reliable sense of optimism about humanity and our future. His research was inspired by another book, published in 1994 by Norbert Elias called; *The Civilizing Process*.

In *The Civilizing Process*, Elias describes how we transition from savage primate to an acceptable, liked, popular, or even celebrated, citizen of our community or the world. He presents a case, not for free-will, but rather for, free-won't.

We are, in essence, a biological community of trillions of single-cell creatures who have organised themselves into clusters of purposeful communities, which create what we describe as organs of the body;, from bones to eyes, lungs and our skin. Freud spoke of instinctive primal drives that lurk in the subconscious and direct our thoughts and behaviour without our knowing, as if the community of cells have agendas and make decisions without us consciously knowing. To a certain extent, this is how it is. Each thought we have is the biproduct of a neural activity; a neuron reaching a synaptic gap and then crossing the gap; as one thought crosses over to another; each thought holding an image, a sentient experience (feeling or emotion) and a narrative (internal voicing or words, whether consciously known or not), the neuron/thought, does not 'select;' which way to go, but rather, it is a deselction process. Norbert reports how, for example, the civilising process is an act of voluntary self-inhibition. All mammals produce spittle, but when, if at all, is it appropriate to spit ?

We mammalians at birth are an oganic unit comprised of an input and output of gooey stuff. We bring nutrients in, process them; metabolise them and eject the toxins from the cell, or out of the system. Sasportas points out that this natural processing is brought to a halt with our first learned, taught, imposed inhibition; potty training.

Potty training is our first dispensation to society. We stop being our innate, natural selves and instead step into being an adapted self; we are no longer content to merely inject and expel, no ! ... we now accept there is a context of place, and a context of time; both of which tell us that is we are to be accepted, then we have to expel our toxins in a certain way, in a certain place and at a certain time - and if we fail to do these things then we may be unacceptable; to our mother, our father, the family, the communist, the clan, the tribe, humanity or even unacceptable to god.

We are faced with a behavioural dilemma:

Adapt and be considered acceptable = you are 'good', you will continue to be fed and watered and protected = you will live.

or ...

Refuse to adapt and be considered to be ill or unwell, or awkward, or belligerent, or 'too much trouble'; you may stop being fed and cared for and protected = you will die.

The drive to conform to the needs of our family and culture are so strong that most humans are encouraged to perform a sense of self adjustment, a voluntary action of self-inhibition, of self-adjustment, of self-discipline, in order to appeal to the larger group and to perhaps become a salient member of the group.

When we chose to direct the expulsion of our toxins in a manner specifically directed by and agreed with those around us, and especially with those in power, we have taken our first steps into becoming civilised; a voluntarily adapted self.

We are no longer being 'who we naturally are as a biological organism ', but rather, 'who we are not. The Neuroscientist Daniel Dennet describes a neuron's orientation in a similar way; it is not that we choose which train of thought to take, but rather, that a process of deselection takes place. In 'The Actor's Brain', Spence describes this processing as, free-won't, rather than, 'free-will'.

If we are passing a bank and notice the doors have been left open; we do not walk past in order to be a good citizen, but rather, walk past because we are taking active steps in stopping ourselves from being a thief. It is not that we are socially passive, but rather that we actively choose to stop ourselves from molesting anyone who takes our fancy. We are exercising free-won't, rather than, free-will.

This dynamical process, across all levels of the human condition, is the root of soul learning on planet Earth. If we are evolving, if we are elevating to some kind of higher consciousness, then the only way to achieve this is to elevate the default condition of the human heart, in such a way, that when faced with challenges, our innate instinct is to err towards kindness, compassion, forgiveness, tolerance, wisdom and love.

Relating with other humans in Earth school isn't all just stick with no carrot though, there is also something to be gained.

In *The Selfish Gene*, Dawkins describes the phenomena of Altruism. Evolutionary psychologists, like Hawkes, suggest that selfless acts are less driven by a desire to help others and more by a social need to be seen by others as being of essential help to others.

Whether it is self, or socially, driven, the behaviour is similar; we behave in small or large societies as if being considered a significant part or player in that society or social narrative is crucial to our ongoing survival and perhaps even to our sense of identity.

It seems that our success, or failure, to attain and maintain a sense of social significance within a society to which we desire inclusion plays a significant role in shaping and colouring our sense of self, the calibre of our self worth and self esteem, our sense of identity and the goals or aspirations we hold; the dreams and spiritual heights to which we aspire.

Aiming towards a specific goal, and consistently behaving in ways which further one's progress towards that goal, is a pathway to achievement and what may be considered success in life.

Successful people often describe both hours of dedication in developing their idea, business or skill and they may also describe the things, usually personal or emotional, which were sacrificed in order to reach their goal, status or achievement.

Sasportas states, the word sacrifice has its roots in the concept of making something sacred. This is often done by giving something of value away, or up, to a 'higher authority'; a Goddess, an ambition, a family member, a social position, a dream or Time. Giving something up that the self values in order to achieve something that the self values even more highly is the very essence of Soul-learning in Earth School.

In a sense, being incarnated may be seen as something akin to doing time in a celestial asylum, in which the Gods employ experiences of temporary pain like electric shock treatment for the soul; a kind of spiritual aversion therapy which encourages us to err towards a default position of wisdom and compassion in our inner most heart. We may behave towards another soul in an unkind way and then experience challenging consequences. We may do this repeatedly until we begin to associate the challenges with the behaviour and consciously discern a sense of consequence. A process of learning cause and effect, not with the conscious mind but with the heart; which means the lessons must run deep ... so deep, that they survive the bridge at the end of life and come with us beyond death into the deep learning of the soul.

This is not, necessarily, a joyful playground; this is Earth School

Pathways of Soul learning

the value of kindness, love, forgiveness and joy

in contrast with the lessons of hatred, revenge and retribution.

Although I have been a teacher of Astrology and Esoteric Studies for 25 years, I have a longer history of conducting and teaching the art of Past Life Regression.

At the beginning of a workshop I ask the participants about their beliefs on past lives and what they believe we may have to live many lives for. Almost universally there is a consensus:

We are a Soul incarnated into human form for the purpose of leaning lessons.

These lessons are designed to enable us to grow in soul-maturity and grow closer to enlightenment; to master everything there is to know on planet Earth cannot be accomplished in a single lifetime, hence the need to repeatedly return and one day become a prefect of this world; and move onto being a newbie in the next realm 'up'.

There are many religions which describe some kind of judgement at the end of this life. The most commonly known are the Abrahamic religions; Judaism, Christianity and Islam. These desert religions partially have their theological roots in an older desert religion known as Zoroastrianism. Zoroaster was the first person to propose that an external judgement takes place after our life here has finished. He was also the first person to suggest that there is a war between light and dark. Before Zoroastrianism life was largely viewed through a lens of animism; there was sunshine and clouds, and laughter and decay and life and death and anger and thunder and these were just things of life; there wasn't a sense of some kind of sinister plot behind the ups and downs of life. Life was just up and down. The cycles of life and death, of birth and re-birth, were just natural and ever constant.

The Abrahamic Religions hold the view that we have just one, and after our one-life is over we wait for the time of judgement when all Souls will either enter heaven and paradise or hell and damnation.

This strand of religious systems have sets of rules that guide their believers on Earth in the behaviour that will go towards ensuring their guaranteed place in 'the good place' later. Most of these rules are stated as negated commands: eg. don't kill, don't steal etc. This causes their believers to be reminded of stealing and killing, by bringing the 'sin' to their attention (negated command: *'don't think of a big blue dog with yellow stripes'* ... what did you just think of)?

Buddhism, for example, is completely different. Certain Buddhist schools of thought have a concept of multiple lives, while others focus on the development of the self in a more humanistic way. Generally Buddhism states its 'rules for good living' in positive language: *'relax more deeply inside now'*, *'be gentle'*, *'allow each and everyone the freedom to follow their own path'*, *'value all life as sacred'* etc. This causes their followers to be reminded of gentleness and relaxing more deeply now ...

There are many variations of polytheistic spiritual approaches such a Pantheonism and Paganism. They often share a common ground of viewing the Soul as a fragment of a great spirit which is learning and adventuring through multiple lives; evolving into a being of enlightened perfection.

One Pagan perspective is described in the Egyptian *book of the dead*. In *Egyptian Religion*, Sir A E Wallis Budge describes a process of self judgement. At the end of each life, a conclusion is drawn about our current level of Self-Mastery that is not so much a statement of condemnation, or congratulation, but rather, is an objective description of what just-is. If we are progressing well, then it is right and true to say that we are progressing well – and it is good to feel good about ourselves.

If there is further work for us to do, then we will create a plan and proceed with the next-life plan at the most optimum moment after a period of further healing, rest and play in the realm of the highest light (some people may call this realm, 'Heaven'). For some newly ascended Souls (recently died) they might find they have manoeuvred themselves into such a state of dis-harmony they require a great deal of patient effort to re-balance and find inner peace once more.

The following diagram depicts the ancient Egyptian view of a Soul's experience after we have departed from this realm.

the weighing of the Soul ~ the Egyptian book of the dead

When the Soul has returned home after life here has ended, and become separated from the deeds and identity of this life, we are then taken into the hall of Maati – a place of rightness and truth. Here, in the presence of the God Osiris, our Soul (often depicted as a heart, or a Soul in a bottle) is placed upon the great scales. On the other scale there is a feather.

The purpose is to see how 'light' we are, by contrasting our Soul with a feather. If we are as light as the feather at the end of the process, we are 'of the light' and can remain in the realms of light and loving beauty. We may progress onto the next level of 'soul-school', or elect to return to Earth as a living guide for other souls on the path. If we are heavier, even by a fraction, than the feather then we must return to Earth school for more lessons; around and around until we have learned to make our heart light with wisdom.

Maat, who knows all things, sits upon the scale while the soul is lead into the chamber by Anubis; the gatekeeper kneeling down. Here Thoth is the record keeper, the scribe who simply records the outcome. Linguistically, the name Thoth appear to be similar to Tora, Tarot , truth and thought.

Within the hall of Maati there are also 42 other deities; Gods and Godesses. We then speak to each one in turn and declare statements about our behaviour while incarnated on Earth as if they are utterly true. However, if we make a pledge and it turns out we are not speaking the truth then, well – let's see …

Just imagine for a moment, you are in a place where there are 42 big people who have all been watching a video of the life you have just finished. On this video, not only have they watched every detail of everything you have said, done and muttered under your breath, they have also been attuned to your private thoughts and feelings – and all the consequences of all you have done, the ripples you have impressed upon the Earth like footprints caste in indelible sand. The Gods know absolutely everything about you.

One by one, you are going to address them and declare out-loud statements about the life you have just finished - as if they are utterly true. You are sitting on a scale in perfect balance as you begin.

Firstly you are called to say the following …. and just imagine how you would feel, right now, if you said aloud, to people who knew you utterly well,

'I have never slain another man'.

How do you feel saying that out-loud ?

Are your feelings affected by saying this out-loud to someone who knows you very well ?

How do you feel ?

Do you become heavier than the feather ?

You may find yourself unaffected by saying that particular statement regarding slaying a person and either feel good or neutral.

Excellent ! … only another 41 to go !

Now, the second statement, and say this out-loud while imagining you are being watched by lots of people who know you very very well:

'I have never allowed my heart to burn with anger'.

How do you feel with that one?

sinking a little lower than the feather? – whoooops, better luck next time.

And now, how about:

'I have never set my mouth in motion against another person'

'Oooooooooouuuuch !'

I like the ancient Egyptian account of what happens after we leave life and return home. The 'Judgement' is self assessment and very comprehensive. It covers far more ground than the 10 rules that some other religions follow and if you were to achieve it all you really would be a most remarkable being.

We haven't the space here to list all 42, but I would highly recommend researching the complete list; the book *Egyptian Religion* by AE Budge I referred to earlier is a good starting point. The list of declarations is extensive and spans our conduct spiritually, and practically, in relationships society, philosophy and conflict. We are called to declare that we have never even once spoke against God; Gods, Goddesses, the Higher Spirit within, your Inner Mind, Higher Self, Etc.) nor cursed the king (highest leader of your land), nor committed theft of any kind. You have not been imperious, or haughty or violent, or wasteful, or hasty in your deeds, or a hypocrite; never crafty, or angry, or avaricious, or fraudulent, or deaf to pious words, or a party to evil (dis-harmonious) actions, or proud, or puffed-up. You have terrified no man, you have not polluted or poisoned your body (alcohol, smoke etc), you have not cheated or soiled any part of your environment.

If that really was a truthful and accurate description of 'You' what would your self-worth and confidence now be like?

It is very extensive and I know I personally have rather a long way to go ...

One of the things I often describe to participants of Past Life Regression workshops is that when we look back at earlier versions of ourselves there is a high chance we may encounter a memory of a less evolved self. This is not who we are now, of course, but if we are kind and considerate, tolerant and compassionate, then we must have learned to become so; and that means we have lifted ourselves out from a primal savagery. Looking back, one may find oneself being murdered, or being a murderer, being raped, or being a rapist; dealing with life on one end of the abuse of power, and in another life, experiencing the dynamics the other way around.

There we are one day, on top of battlements during a medieval siege, pouring boiling oil over the heads of people below at the base of the castle wall, and if we might meet one of the next week in a library. If we are unlucky, they may recognise us and be overwhelmed with an urge to repeatedly throw books at us, while their horrified partner cannot understand why they are compelled to attack a nice stranger.

Not all encounters have a past-life dynamic, of course; we often meet new people for the first time, but they may be an underlying background behind the dynamics of certain relationships we form with partners, family members, in-laws, friends, team mates, chums or work colleagues which seem to have an emotional intensity which is disproportionate to how we have been interacting with them.

Sometimes, we may encounter someone and find the hairs on the back of our hand stand on end. Sometimes, we may find that even though we are happily married, we are swept away by a passion which turns our very life and identity upside down. If you cannot understand a relationship from looking at the surface, then you may need to explore more deeply.

Reincarnationists hold the view that powerful emotional bonds survive the separation of death at the end of life and connection between the two souls continues, like timeless astral elastic. These emotional bonds are not necessarily loving or pleasant; they may possibly be unpleasant and conflicts between souls may take many lifetimes to resolve.

Belief in reincarnation and continuum of the Soul can be traced further back than ancient Egypt, and for those who adopt this philosophical relationship with life certain dynamics of living become easier to manage. It also has a pitfall or two for those who do not consider things deeply; 'a little knowledge ... '

In a later chapter we are going to explore the nature of words and narrative and the important role words play in creating our relationship with life and ourselves. Before we reach that point I'd like to have a brief discussion about three words which relate with reincarnation; Think ... Believe .... Know.

When we think something, we are still engaged in the process of forming a conclusion, which means we are undecided.

'Do you love him?' 'I think so ...' . Hmmm ...

'I think you are beautiful'. Really, are you not sure?

When we believe something, we desire it to be so.

When we know something, we are confident, steadfast, and sound in our conviction.

When participants arrive for a past life regression workshop, if it is a new experience for them, they begin the day either in the position of thinking there may be something in it, or of desiring confirmation of their belief. When a participant experiences a memory of a life they have lived before this one coming into mind, they transition into the state of Knowing.

While the content of the memories holds the conscious attention of the participants; where were you? what did you do? what was it like? ; a subtle and yet powerful change takes place within the core of the participant's relationship with life and what it is to be a human being.

The Deepack Chopra saying, 'We are not human beings having a spiritual experience, but spiritual beings having a human experience', describes this new relationship with life perfectly. To know, not just believe, but to Know that every person you love will not completely go away; that you will meet again and the longest time you may experience the sense of being separated in consciousness is perhaps a human lifetime; 90-ish years at the most; a blink of an eye to an ancient tree. Knowing, with complete certainty, that you will meet again anyone with whom you have formed an affectional bond, makes dealing with loss and bereavement much easier than it is for those who are not living in the state of knowing. It also makes one's own mortality easier to consider and has powerful influence on one's life, behaviour, moral code and our conduct in personal relationships. To know that each step you take is impressing itself upon a moment in time up ahead when you meet your own deeds, and all of the ripples of consequences which radiate out from ourselves and our actions, is a sobering, and inspiring thought.

Certain cultures and religions follow a philosophy of, 'an eye for an eye', meaning that a sense of justice is sought on this Earth plane by doing to a person exactly what that person has themselves done. The seeking of retribution in this way may take place in private within a family or a relationship, or more publically in a group, a gang, a society or may even be sanctioned by the state and codified in the laws of the land. From a Reincarnationist perspective, such acts of retribution or revenge create more problems than they seek to resolve. Since every detail of everything we do is impressed upon the essence of Spirit and waits for us up ahead at the end of life, every criminal is already on their way to meet a justice they cannot escape from. If we act out behaviours of revenge, we inadvertently also initiate new cycles of problems for ourselves in the future. Souls need to learn, and like stopping a child from running into the road, sometimes the state needs to address a person's savage behaviour and enact a punishment judged in a court, in accord with the wishes of society. When done with justice and compassion for all parties concerned, punishment alongside a desire for reform enters the realm of what may be termed, 'reparation', or restorative justice.

 The desire for justice to be conducted within this lifetime, so that it is 'seen to be done', is understandable from the perspective of the conscious mind. As far as the conscious mind is concerned, 'now' is the only time there is.

Viewing a Soul's journey across eons of time, the dynamics of justice and learning take on a broader view.

This may be unpleasant to consider, and I apologise for any discomfort a reader may experience, but in order to illustrate what I mean, I have to mention something unpleasant. Imagine a scenario in which there are two souls incarnated in human form hundreds of years ago. One is incarnated as a male, and the other as a female. During this imagined life time, centuries ago, the soul that is incarnated as a male humans rapes the female. A heinous and dreadful thing to do. From a Soul's perspective, not only is an attack violent and repugnant, a violation of one's very being, it also forces that Soul onto a path not of their choosing.

From an eye for an eye perspective, it would be 'fair' if the Soul that was raped has the opportunity to rape the rapist, to enact revenge and plunge them onto a path not of their choosing. However, Souls learn many things and Earth school has more than just one dynamic, more than one season, more than one colour to its sky.

The two Souls in our story incarnate at the beginning of the 21st century in the same geographical space; and place known as 'London'. Each Soul has incarnated as the opposite gender to the one they expressed all those centuries ago; the man is now a woman, and the woman is now a man. By prior Soul-arrangement, organised during the pre life planning stage into which all possible pathways are woven, they have each found themselves driven to live near the same London park and have a love of dogs.

One evening both Souls decide to take their dogs for a walk at the same time, in the same place; a large London park. It was one of those evenings in late October when the changing season's mist hangs heavy in the evening air, making the sky almost feel as if it is low on the ground and people shuffle past one another as if walking in their own silent world.

The two Souls, unconsciously guide the feet of their body to the same quiet area of parkland. As they begin to approach one another, their state of consciousness begins to subtly change, almost as if they are in a tunnel-vision dream-like state. The Soul that was once a woman and is now a man is thinking about sex a lot and is half-aware of feeling energised and aroused. The Soul that was once a man and is now a woman is half-aware of feeling somewhat subdued and yet also vulnerable. As they approach, they momentarily make eye contact and there is a faint flicker of recognition.

In the centuries since they last met, the Soul that was a woman who was raped was ushered onto pathways of learning that it did not choose. The Soul had many adventures; on the seas of the world, in the deep forest as a hermit and even as the wife of a tribal leader. The experiences of living through different lenses of power has taught the Soul how it feels to be a recipient of another person's tyranny and also to be tyrannical oneself. Over many lifetimes the Soul has learned the arts of forgiveness and compassion and grown in wisdom.

As the bodies of the two Souls become within arms reach of one another, the Soul that is now animating a male body forgives the other, and they silently pass one another with a nod of exchange. The Soul that is now female feels not just a sigh of relief but also the lifting of a centuries old cloud of guilt lifting away. It is as if the weight of the burden has been dispelled.

Earth school is not an arena for the conscious mind's learning, nor even for the human heart. It is a school for Souls, and learning is the Soul's purpose.

The Soul that once raped another learns exactly the same lessons; the same intensity of wisdom from being forgiven as it would from being attacked. From a Soul perspective, there is no difference as far as the depth of Soul-learning goes, except for one very important thing; a new cycle of retribution and counter-revenge has not been set into motion. An olde cycle of heaviness and pain has been brought to an end and *both* Souls are now lighter of heart as a result.

Karma does not mean; 'bad things happen to you because you have been bad in the past'.

Another ill-thought rumour regarding reincarnation is the idea that, 'a person who had a disability is disabled because they are being punished for being wicked in a past life'. An England football manager was once sacked for expressing this inaccurate belief and a British soap star caused outrage among disabled people for expressing a similar view. This viewpoint is the conclusion drawn from scant information and a narrow view.

It may be possible that a Soul is experiencing hardship as a consequence of past behaviour, of course, but, it is also possible that a Soul is experiencing hardship for other reasons.

We always find something new more difficult to master than something we are well versed in. A Soul could be experiencing new challenges, new circumstances, and find things difficult as a result.

A Soul may also be experiencing difficulties in order to learn lessons more swiftly. Like a fast-track pathway, a Soul may elect to undertake 3-lifetimes of pain by being born with autism or cerebral palsy, for example; not to make reparation for past wicked behaviour but rather, to heroically carry additional pain in order to learn deeply and swiftly.

These are just three possibilities for a reason behind a person being born with a physical disability; there are many more. But, even if we have only these three reasons, it means that we can no longer elect just one of them like a default belief; we have to either suspend judgment or investigate the individual's past life history properly.

Souls learn as much from love, laughter and kindness as they do from hardship, gloom and pessimism. We can make ourselves lighter of heart by also helping others to have a lighter heart too. In Social Psychology, Rogers defines Altruism as; 'acting for the benefit of others as an end in itself with no expectation of reward'. Kindness makes us feel good about ourselves; we have a lighter heart and a deeper learning in this Earthly school for Souls.

Dynamics of relating

3 lenses of love: Unconditional love, caring, romance - connecting

In the psychological model of in Carl Jung there are the two primary anthropomorphic archetypes of the unconscious. The anima and animus are described as elements of the collective unconscious, a domain of the unconscious that transcends the personal psyche and to which we are all attuned. Jung often looked at the conscious and unconscious as a polarity of expression. For example, if a person were expressing logic, they may be suppressing their feelings in that moment. Conversely, if a person is expressing emotions, they are suppressing logic at that moment in time. Jung helps a similar orientation towards male and female principles. Please remember, these are archetypical in nature and not correlated with gender or masculinity or femininity. In the book, *The Soul Map*, Murry Stein reports that Jung proposed that the unconscious of a man holds the archetypal images of the eternal feminine, the Anima, which, when connected with the ego and collective unconscious may potentially open a pathway to knowing the Self. Animas, equivalently, are the archetypal images of the eternal masculine that a woman holds within her unconscious which, when connected with the ego and collective unconscious may potentially open a pathway to knowing the Self.

In *The Twelve Houses*, Howard Sasportas extends the principle of the Anima even further by correlating anima with three symbols from Astrology; Neptune, The Moon and Venus.

In my Astrological teachings i hold the view that these three symbols each represent a different element in the feminine dynamics of human love.

Neptune represents that part of us which is spiritual and loves soul-to-soul. From a purely spiritual perspective, all souls love one another. We souls are, if you like, cells in the body of light which some call 'God', and, as such love and care for the divinity and well being and integrity of all souls, no matter whether they are in astral form or incarnated into a form of life in a Soul-school, like Earth. Neptune represents the human capacity for unconditional love which finds its brightest wings in a spiritual context.

I have observed over the years in the news feeds of social media, that people who have attended certain workshops, or read certain books, mostly of a new age philosophy, make public a desire for unconditional love in their lives.

To be loved consistently, without waver would be wonderful; like basking in an eternal summer. What a delight for the Soul, for the heart, this would be ... or, would it ?

To experience life as if the season have stopped turning would not be to experience life at all; life would be on pause; a living death. Beyond life, there is a return home and much learning and the most beautiful loving joy. What we call 'death', the end of life, is not stagnation; it is a liberation into a more beautiful and profound existence. Stagnation is death; life on pause and a relentless entrapment in time; this would be a living end.

To desire unconditional love in one's human relationships is potentially dangerous. To have an unyielding love for someone if they stamp on your toes, to continue loving someone unconditionally even after they spit in your food, rape your sister or steal all that you own. Perhaps what some people mean is that they wish to be loved without any condition of what *they* do, or how *they* treat the other person; 'whether I am nice to you or not, you shall continue to consistently love me', 'whether I am supportive in this hour of your need, or not, you must continue to consistently love me'.

To me, this is not a very enlightened perspective.

If I may use one of the above crude examples, to say; 'you spat in my food while we were in Earth school and I was aghast and didn't like you then, but now we have left light and are once more in our Soul-state, I can appreciate what I learned about myself and how I relate with others and the world, so thank you for that my wonderful soul companion'.

When we are in our soul-state, we are unencumbered by the particular lens we have of life through our human psyche and the weight of our heart; we see everything and everyone clearly and everyone is of the light.

From our Earthly perspective, a rapist, a concentration camp guard, a deceptive politician a bullying husband are seen as 'horrible', and rightly so. We are in school here, and it is by discerning that which is acceptable and favourable, from that which is hurtful and best avoided; the difference between wisdom and folly, that we grow in light from the shadows we find here towards our place in the light of an eternal spiritual sun.

Unconditional love is Soul stuff, not heart stuff, and being aware of the difference can reduce a lot of unnecessary pain in life.

Soul-to-Soul then, I love you, dear reader, I deeply really do. From lifetime to lifetime, in whichever ways we have connected; that my heart is able to reach out to yours in friendship, kindness and love right now is truly wonderful. May I thank you for your time here; for your appreciation and joy as these words fly from this page into the heart of your mind.

That part of us that cares that nurtures and protects; whether a mother with a child, a doctor with a patient, a warden with an otter, a vet with a beloved family pet; we care. We have evolved an altruism which extends beyond our family unit, our clan, our tribe, our nation, culture and even our species.

In Astrology, the symbol form this nurturing, caring part is called The Moon. we look at the condition of the Moon, meaning its Sign and House and Aspects (angles) to all other Planets and parts of the Chart, and the Houses touched by the sign Cancer, to represent the polysemous layers of experience of caring dynamics of an individual. These dynamics are initiated in the first three years of life; especially from nurturing experiences with the person's mother, or 'primary caregiver, and then often extend out across the person's entire life span.

The combinations of nurtured experiences in our formative years colour both how we nurture others and how we ourselves wish to be nurtured. Whichever nurturing style you have formed in your unconscious, your unconscious will conspire to bring into your life those very same conditions, however, the context in which we find ourselves will adapt and modify how it manifests in behaviour. If we were always given a treat when we were upset, such as a toy or a sweet, then when we are in the company of someone who is upset, we will instinctively wish to give them something or some kind of treat; 'never mind love, 'ave a cup of tea'. If we are upset, we may feel uncomfortable, or feel, 'something is wrong', if a cup of tea is not offered. If, when we were young, someone always sat with us and told us stories which broadened our sense of what the present upset 'means', we may find ourselves counselling others, affording their fleeting moment of eternal darkness a broader and brighter and more hopeful illumination. We may feel somewhat 'flat', if there is no one around to chat and talk us out of the midnight blues.

Our drive to nurture and care seems innate. We are drawn to help our fellow Earthlings by social constructs we find around us or by internal drives engendered from lives lived before this one or the conditioning, or scripting, we have received here in this one. In the broad spectrum of the human condition, caring styles can range from deep compassion to dissociated indifference. It can be illuminating to be aware of one's own nurturing style.

The Third symbol one may borrow from Astrology to represent a dynamic of love is Venus; romantic love. In mythology Venus, the Goddess of love, sweetness and light is also envious, judging and possessive. In romantic love, we have a certain taste and style and it is natural that we seek a partner with whom we can relate well. In my client work over the years I have found people seem to forget that the word, 'relationship', has the word, 'relate', embedded within it. The more we can relate with someone with our temperament, disposition, beliefs, values, outlook, ideology, humour, artistic tastes and styles, the closer we come to finding a deeper quality of compatibility.

Objectively, it would be true to say that every person in the world is beautiful - Everyone.

Every creature is beautiful too; every giraffe, worm, salmon and warthog. Mr Warthog might not be beautiful to us, it would be strange if he were, by Mrs Warthog likes him, and that's what matters. Likewise with people. Attraction is highly subjective and it changes over time; a person we may find attractive when we are 19 may be different to who catches our eye when we are 57. As we journey through time and experience highs and lows, gaining new insights and bruises, the qualities we look for and desire may also change over time. It is not always the case, of course; it is personal, subjective and uniquely individual.

There is something about how we humans relate with the world that may be useful to take into account when we are considering the somewhat turbulent realm of romance and emotion.

We navigate reality by attempting to understand what is happening, and what we are encountering, and then forming a decision about how best to respond and react, given our comprehension of the situation and an intended direction or goal we may already have in mind. Our nervous system feeds information from the world around us into our brain through sights, sounds, feelings, smells, tastes. Proprioception, temperature and the social environment, internal processing needs such as homeostatic equilibrium, hunger, thirst, ease, comfort, pain, fear, adventure and other affective dynamics, combine to create a sense of 'now'. What we need to do then, in less than a second, is take all these signals into account and conduct; 'the making of meaning'. Being able to accurately comprehend phenomena is vital for being able to conduct oneself in safety, let alone achieve success. If we form the opinion that a moving car is stationary, it may be the last opinion we are able to form.

The process by which we comprehend what we subjective experience as 'reality' is highly complex. The words we use to describe our subjective experience plays a very large role in determining our relationship with what we encounter. Native speakers of English are inclined to describe subjective in a way which is different from its objective reality. For example, if we see a red book we may describe it as a 'red book'. This is obvious, of course, however; the book is not red. In *The Structure of Magic*, Bandler and Grinder illustrate this illusionary use of language. The book is absorbing ever colour of the spectrum of visible light except for red; red is the name we give to the portion of the light spectrum which is being deflected from the object. The reality is, it is a non-red book. We mis-describe other things in life too. For example, you may believe you have seen a sunrise or a sunset, but you have never seen a sun set, because the sun does not set. We are revolving around it, and what we are really witnessing is the Earth turning to the east. It would be culturally strange though to say, 'I saw a fabulous turning to the east tonight darling, the colours were astonishing'.

A similar mis-reading of meaning takes place when someone say a person is beautiful.

When we say, 'you are beautiful', it sounds as if the quality of beauty is owned by the person we are referring to. But this is not the case. Objectively, like Mr Warthog, every person is intrinsically beautiful, as a member of the human family. However, we do not say, 'you are beautiful', to absolutely everyone we encounter. We tend to reserve these words for only a few of the 7 billion. When we say, 'you are beautiful', we really mean; 'because of the natured and nurtured beliefs, values, likes, preferences, artistic styles I have come to love and value, in the context of my present circumstances, I am easily able to see the beauty in you'. In other words, the beauty is not experienced as something which belongs to the person receiving the compliment, but rather, it is being perceived inside the person declaring the compliment. The experience of the beauty is subjective, and this is what is meant by the figure of speech; 'Beauty is in the eye of the beholder'.

Whether someone considers us to be beautiful or not, we are still beautiful anyway. Our desire to be desired by a specific person may not be quite so philosophical and we may experience painful emotions if we feel rejected.

Romance is highly subjective and very conditional. We want to be loved in a way that suits us. What suits one person may not suit another; some people like kindness while others get a thrill from sarcasm. For some people, if there is an absence of arguments or even violence then, 'it ain't love', while others yearn for a life of gentle, loving care. Sometimes, we may find we are a paradoxical mixture of things and life can become confusing and muddled.

In early 21st century western spiritual culture, a popular model, or framework, for understanding the nature of our relationship with life was, *'The Law of Attraction'*. This belief system espouses the view that whatever we 'are', or rather, whatever 'energy' we resonate with, draws towards us that which reflects or resonates with our present 'vibration'.

Beliefs from other systems of thought hold a similar understanding. Towards the end of the 20th century, the discovery of *Mirror Neurons*, revealed the brain mechanism with which one person is able to perceive and comprehend the experience of another person and empathically, 'feel what you feel'.

In the 18th century Franz Mesmer proposed his theories of *Animal Magnetism*, suggesting that an invisible 'force' passes between all people, which has the capacity to contract and expand and change in 'tone' or 'quality'. He called this; *Rapport*.

Whichever of these narratives we prefer to follow, there is a similar conclusion; we relate with the world around us by tuning in to certain dynamics of all that may be possible while excluding other possibilities. Certain qualities have salience in our attention, while others remain in the background. imagine your attention; both conscious and unconscious, intellectual and emotional, spiritual and sentient, operates like a mixing desk in a studio, or frequency bands on a graphic equaliser. Certain frequencies, such as bass, might be set to maximum, and treble set to minimum. Attention has flexibility and variety; on another occasion it might be treble which is salient, or at maximum, and bass which is held in the background.

At the moment of meeting another person with whom we will share time and experience in a bond of mutual love, we form a special kind of relationship. The quality of that relationship is proportional to the quality of how deeply we are able to relate with that person in that, and each following, moment in time.

To me, it seems that all souls are on pathways of converging and diverging.

In 2006 I had no idea that Facebook existed; no idea that I would write 'notes' on various dynamics of love and post them for thousands to enjoy, no idea that the comments of appreciation from people would sow the origins of this book you are reading right now, and yet, every footstep. Every beat of our hearts was leading towards the moment of you reading these words I am writing now. In 2006, we were living our lives on our unique individual pathways, and yet we were also on a path of coming together.

I hold the view that all souls converge, travel together along a parallel path for a period of time and then diverge again away from one another again when whatever exchange or learning to be done is done; or, until one of the people changes in some way at a faster rate than the other.

As Stephen Fry once said in an address at an iTunes festival, 'We are not nouns, we are verbs'. We change as we journey through time; we learn, we grow, some would say we evolve; and therefore, what suits us changes as we move through time.

At a point in time when we find we can relate well with another person, that capacity to relate is not carved in stone, it is changeable. We meet and walk a parallel path; this may be for a very short amount of time, like 30 seconds, or for a much longer period over many lifetimes.

Sometimes the condition of our inner state changes with a rapid and repeating frequency; our changing moods. If our moods change with great depth, how we relate, and who we are able to relate with may also change along with the rise and fall of our changes. In *The Actor's Brain*, Spence shows that our identity is dependent upon our ability to recall who we are in the context of our autobiographical history. Rossi refers to a phenomena called, *State Dependent Memory*, which describes how our moods, or state, predetermines which memories we can access and which memories fall into amnesia . What is salient for us will change with changes in deep mood and we may even seem to be different in character with each oscillation. Some people have an oscillation time of minutes, even seconds. For others it is hours or days, and for others years, decades or a lifetime. We may meet people who have the same manner about them for years and years, keeping to the same routine and holding the same views irrespective of how the world around them appears to change.

When we meet a person whose state changes are in synchrony with ours, we are better able to relate with them. Better relating is even more assured if, when we change, we both travel in the same direction.

'they were fine until'

... he discovers rally driving on rainy afternoons, or, she finds herself on a spiritual retreat and begins speaking with different frames of reference that he doesn't fully understand. We converge and grow closer, and, we also diverge and grow further apart. When we meet, what we find in the alchemy of love is a degree of compatibility that is constellated in that moment. Once one of the partners change at a rate which is faster than the other, or in a different direction regarding philosophy, religion, politics, life-style, manor of self-expression or values etc, then the level of compatibility changes and the alchemy may change from that of romance to friendship or friendship to romance, or romance to deeper commitment; there are numerous pathways and possibilities, each with their own value and lessons of learning for the Soul.

Some souls do a diamond shape and, like souls attached to astral elastic, converge-diverge-converge-diverge ...

The speed of oscillation may wax and wane through an afternoon of close-distance, close-distance, or it may be a longer cycle of lifetime together-lifetime separate, lifetime together-lifetime separate, lifetime together ...

Perhaps, if rejection is ever a problem, rather than thinking that it is 'you that is wrong', it is nothing more than a question of bumping into someone you like at a moment in time when it is not fortuitous for that particular love to grow.

Sometimes, we may meet someone we like but there is an age difference - time problem.

Sometimes we may meet someone and there is a circumstance issue: space problem.

If the bonds of mutual liking are strong enough, circumstances will rarely stop feet from finding one another, though sometimes it may be culturally politically dangerous; like crossing a gang, class, race or religious divide.

Describing the process of meeting and then navigating the dynamics of relating changes is one thing, but what about the concerns some people have of being unsuccessful in relationships. 'I can't do relationships, perhaps they are not meant to happen for me'.

Every relationship has its ending built inside its beginning. This doesn't mean we are all 'destined' to part company; at some time up ahead, one partner will die and leave life. Even if both partners return home at the same time, their earthly relationship has come to an end. To me, it seems that to attempt to evaluate a relationship on its length-of-time is to miss the point; like trying to evaluate the quality of sleep by clock-time. One can sleep for 4 hours and wake refreshed on one occasion, and at another time, sleep for ten hours and wake up still exhausted. Like everything emotional, sleep and love are best comprehended for their quality of depth, rather than for their numerical quantity of clock-time.

The quality of a relationship is best measured, or comprehended, by the depth of the feeling; the frequency of heartfelt smiles, the brightness and warmth of our joy together. Love is truly a beautiful and wonderful thing. It has many colours and depths, and each may have different enduring qualities.

When a romantic relationship comes to the end of its time, although the couple have stopped relating on a Venusian level, they may still continue relating on a Moon and Neptune level. This can seem confusing. A person may say, 'I do not love you', meaning, 'I no longer love you in a romantic context', but the person listening may instinctively sense that the spiritual soul-connection is still intact and may find themselves thinking that the person saying 'I no longer love you' is wrong or even attempting to perform a deception. The antidote to a confusion is clarity. By clearly stating the context in which we love someone; as 'just a friend', 'soul explorers', 'like family', 'romantic lovers', etc, it is easier for both people to find in which ways they share common ground and where there are differences in what each desires at that time.

It is healthier to be honest and clear than to be nervous of expressing oneself or fearful of causing a divergence. Finding someone with whom we can relate in a deep and heartfelt way seems to be easy for some people and yet fraught with anxiety, pessimism or even a 'fated' cynicism for others.

In the 1988 book, *Finding Each Other*, John Selby describes a meditational process for finding one's 'soul mate', or at least, bringing the moment of meeting your next love closer, sooner in time. The first half of the book featured exercises to heal and repair emotional history; to cleanse the heart ready for your new love to step inside. When you are ready you then begin to make contact across time and space with your new love, who is already on their way to you. This is done in a manner following an ancient hunting ritual. The warrior would, before setting out in pursuit, sit and meditate and 'tune in', to the soul of the animal he is to hunt. The quarry is already hunted in potential, and the warrior would whisper to his prey, soothing and giving thank and gratitude. When he begins hunting, there is already a connection, a bond, and like astral elastic, their feet are drawn together.

For lovers, this dynamic is also true. Right now, the next person you are going to fall in love with is here; yes, they are here, right now, walking upon the surface of the earth.

The technique is to sit in a calm and relaxed state, and imagine a beam of your consciousness can reach out into the ethers and touch their aura. To attract a soul-mate, give them no image, nor detail, nor any sense of physical expectation let their skin colour, culture physique be what it will; you are connecting with Soul.

When you 'feel' you have made contact, whisper, softly, lovingly, say hello ... :)

The act of doing this strengthens the astral soul bond between you and draws you both closer in time to the moment of meeting.

One word of caution though:

Inducing such a moment of meeting may mean that conditions in their life have to change more rapidly than they otherwise may have done, and this may be disruptive. It may also disrupt for your life too. Whether this is morally appropriate or a good thing or a bad thing for all those concerned all depends on the specific context, and that is something only you can decide at heart.

We meet and fall in love; and we love in different ways, in different layers of our being. Being human is a complex business and relating with others can be both a dream and a headache, and sometimes both at once !

34

Relating with other souls in romantic love

Emotional needs, Romance, Commitment and Intimacy

In my couple counselling and relationship astrology work, we focus a spotlight onto 4 primary areas of relating. While the whole of life is important in relationships, from family dynamics, relating with work colleagues and team mates, intimate relationships are viewed through 4 different lenses:

Emotional needs and unconscious conditioning.

Romance.

Commitment.

Intimacy.

Emotional needs and unconscious conditioning.

In the formative years of life we experience the world in a certain way. The family nest we find ourselves in may be close, loving and supportive. Conversely, for some people, the nest they find themselves in may be unsupportive, cold or aggressively dangerous. Sometimes there is a paradoxical mixture; parents might be verbally supportive and encouraging and yet not necessarily physically close or demonstrative; hugs may be at a minimum.

However we find the early home environment, a kind of conditioning takes place within both your unconscious and in your body's sentient relationship with the phenomenological world it experiences; this is both emotional and sentient learning, cognitive and visceral.

The condition, or quality, of the nest we find ourselves in tells us about the world we are immersed in, and we absorb the emotions, narratives, and chemistry which surrounds us. Some people find themselves held in a next of enthusiasm and praise, cleanliness and loving kindness while others may experience abandonment or aggression, abuse, chemical poison or violence. Whether it is happening directly to us or we are witness to dynamics from the spectrum of human expression, it becomes a part of our experience and is laid down among the layers of memories which later comes to form our sense of being; an autobiographical notion of who we are and what we can, and cannot, be. These layers are embedded within our visceral memory systems and what others may describe as the non-conscious. I prefer the term unconscious.

There are various terms used for describing the process, or mechanism, of how our brains absorb these early impressions and how they consequentially change the physical architecture of our brain, and therefore, our thoughts and character (Shore). This process has been called 'imprinting' (Bowlby), 'neuro-associative conditioning' (Robbins), and 'habit' (my Dad).

In *The Selfish Gene*, Richard Dawkins introduced the concept of 'memes', stating that we do not just inherit biological traits but also figures of speech, discourses, 'in-jokes', and modes of comprehension and understanding from our family and cultural backgrounds. Geneticists and biologists such as Lipton and Noble describe 'epigenetics'; genes which are not automatically switched on, such as the colour of your eyes, but lay dormant as potentials within us which are 'experience dependent'. The chemical environment predetermines whether or not the genetic material is read or ignored. Earnest L Rossi reports that one of the key triggering chemicals is glucose and glucose is one of many bi-products of neural activity, or, thoughts ... (for a detailed description of this process please see; *How We Come into Being* - David Charles Rowan).

These formative impressions of life and a sense of 'that which is home', do not just effect us on a personal level, they also impact how we relate in love.

For example, if a baby is distant from mum:

For a long period of time during the first three years of life; whether from being on life support in an incubator or mum has to leave regularly for work, or if a mother feels emotionally distant from her baby, the baby can become accustomed to a sense of space and emotional distance. This does not apply to every baby who begins life in an incubator or who has a working mother, but those who have a propensity to be sensitive to the sense of 'space'. Growing up with an emotional and unconscious need for space and freedom can conflict with other parts of the self which later in life want to form close intimate relationships. How can we be close and yet distant at the same time ?

We could:

Confuse the boundary between friendship and romance and unknowingly attract people who won't fully commit - which then allows us to escape commitment.
Or, find ourselves drawn to people who are physically distant; the live next door, in the next street, town, country or continent!

We might find ourselves attracting people who work strange hours or shift patterns which mean we spend a lot of time alone, for example.

There are many ways that an unconscious need for space can manifest, but with this kind of 'space-dynamic', there is once thing of which we can be certain; if someone with this unconscious drive attempts to live with someone in a small confined apartment they will feel suffocated to the point of exploding like a cork out of a bottle!

What they need is a large house in which she lives in the east wing, he lives in the west wing, and then they only need to figure who has control of the key to the door in the middle. A gentleman, of course, would agree with every lady's answer to that question.

However, because cultures and their emergent societies have developed along conventional, husband-wife coupledom lines, if a person feels comfortable outside of that relating structure and does not have an inner sense of 'permission for diversity', they could find themselves feeling 'odd' or 'strange' or even 'fated to be alone', when all they need is an understanding of their emotional unconscious need for space and freedom. Once we are more aware of our innate nature, we can then more clearly articulate this to another person and more easily find others with the same needs and then connect with people with whom we can relate; relating in relationship.

What might happen if we invert the dynamic; a situation in which a baby is given constant loving attention.

Not every first daughter or first son is impacted by the constant loving attention of parents who revolve around their new child like satellites orbiting a star, but some are. For those who imbibe this initial sense of adoration; school, and further up ahead, work, can seem strangely cold and indifferent. The contrast from being held in warm, consistent attention to a feeling of being ignored can be painful if a person has developed an emotional need for attentive acknowledgement.

This may sound like a recipe for narcissism, but there is another dynamic that is more often the case; creativity. If a person has an unconscious need for attention and they find themselves at an early school, they swiftly learn a few things. Attention can be gained from making a noise, making a scene, making a mess or making a picture or a story. A recognition of the quality of attention can begin to build an aptitude for 'playing to the gallery'. If the 'audience', is class mates, then naughtiness may ensue. If teacher is the target audience though, then an aptitude for creative and artistic expression can produce fantastic works of art, literature or music throughout their life span. If a person develops a prolific output of creativity, one would assume that anyone wishing to form a relationship with them would be a fan of their art, music or writing. For a person whose emotional nature is so entwined with their creativity and the reception towards what they have created, their heart's expression, a cold reception can be experienced like the deep frost of rejection.

Sincerity, congruence and authenticity are different ways of describing what may be termed 'honesty'. The word 'honour' is embedded within the word 'honesty', and when we express ourselves sincerely, congruently and authentically we pay honour to our voice in the symphony of creation. When we give honour to our expression and also have the humility to do so with kindness and compassion, the light we radiate to the world is not just warm and inviting; it may also be healing.

A person with an unconscious need for constant loving attention may demand such attention and step onto a path of conceit, if not narcissism. Alternatively, such an unconscious need may ignite a creative flame worthy of applause from the world and those fortunate enough to share close time in their company.

Some babies learn to find close scrutiny to be rather too painful. For example, a baby that finds itself in a family which , on the one hand, is ship shape and tidy, may also find itself in a next with everyone constantly describing what is wrong, or not right, or not good enough. These conditions may nurture an unconscious need to both find fault and also to be criticised. If they are praised, they wait for the, 'and ...', or the, 'but ... '.

Navigating a world full of people who are 'souls in a working-progress', questing for perfection but not yet arriving, is challenging enough, but when your unconscious is nurtured to, 'fault-find' , the resulting awareness of the incompetence one encounters can be rather uncomfortable. Teachers who do not educate, politicians who do not lead, singers who mime.

An acute propensity for analysis can be useful in certain contexts, such as in the food hygiene department; we need you!

On the other hand, an analysis conducted at the breakfast table can disenchant romance. If someone gives you a rose; taking the petals off it to investigate what it is can mean you are left holding only a thorny stalk.

Perfectionism can be a pathway to beauty if one's philosophy holds the view that everything in nature is an expression of nature's perfection. Humans make fantastic mistakes and brilliant calamities; mistakes are the tools of a Soul's learning. An acceptance of difference, a celebration of diversity and an awareness of the value in all forms of life and human expression can illume the heart that otherwise might tear life into shreds with narratives of 'wrongness' and the pain of ill-met expectations.

'Disappointment requires adequate planning', Richard Bandler.

Disappointment can be a very painful experience. For a person with an unconscious need for perfection it can be heart-wrenching. However, there is something we can do to moderate the possibility of disappointment from taking place. It does not involve lowering our expectations or standards, but rather, checking to ensure our narrative and labels of expectation are accurate.

A useful metaphor for checking, and possibly adjusting, the labels with which we identify and relate with others is the imagery or a sports stadium set up with concentric rings like a dartboard or a tree.

Outside of the stadium are all of the strangers in the world; those we have never met and are unaware of.

In the top outer seating, high up in the stadium, are the seats for Acquaintances; these are the people with whom we have a sense of recognition but still do not know very well. Language is an important part of how we navigate reality; Facebook calls acquaintances friends, when really they are virtual-network connections, until we get to know someone more closely.

I mentioned that language is important. We navigate reality through our senses and internal experience and whenever we encounter phenomena we engage in an activity which may be described as, 'the making of meaning'. Words are not just clusters of sounds with which we convey meaning; they are also symbols of experience.

Chum, mate, pal, friend, good friend, best friend - all of these terms have distinctively different meanings and each of us will have our own unique interpretation. Our relationship with 'reality' is highly subjective and I am not going to define each of these terms here, for that would only give you a 'Rowan view', but it may be worth you considering for a moment; what constitutes a 'good friend', for you ?

If your car breaks down 400 miles from your home, would a chum or a mate come to get you? Would a friend come to your rescue, or indeed, would a good friend come to your aid?

Before we continue with constructing the metaphor I highly recommend that you define for yourself each of these terms so that they are each clear to you.

Radiating from the outer seating, through the stands and onto the pitch itself, have the layers of seating in order of intimacy. For example, Chums, Mates, Pals, Friends, Good Friends, Best Friends.

In the center of the pitch, within the inner circle there is one single chair; this chair is yours. It is very important that, like the sun in the solar system, you are at the heart of your world.
In the rings immediately surrounding the central circle lay the areas for those who are closest to your heart; the realm of your deepest love.

These rings radiate out until they meet the area for your best friends. Your Best Friends area may be close or distant to the rings of Deep Love, depending on how deeply you love your best friends.

Now, to use the metaphor;

In a quiet space, take in a deep breath and relax your shoulders as you now breath out ...

Continue breathing slowly and deeply and imagine you are placing your emotions, your feelings into 'neutral'.

Now, begin to think of the people in your life, one at a time, and allow their feet to automatically walk themselves into the zone or area which naturally suits them for how they relate with you now ...

Watch with a sense of dethatched interest to see who goes where.

You may find everyone sits exactly where you thought they would. On the other hand, there may be some unexpected surprises. There might be someone you consider to be a friend who has for a while been behaving towards you as if they are a mate or a chum. There may be an acquaintance you have recently met who has extended a hand of deep friendship to you.

It can be an interesting exercise to see if the labels that we attribute to the people in our lives match their behaviour towards us in our relationship context.
If someone behaves towards us like a mate, but we incorrectly call them a friend, then their behaviour will cause us to feel a sense of discomfort, or even disappointed or let down. Once we adjust the label to match the current situation we now find their behaviour towards us and manner of relating exactly fits our expectation and we no longer feel 'let down'.

Sometimes, we may find that needing to make a very large adjustment is emotionally painful. This exercise can bring to light a realisation that a dear friend has become distant and such an illumination can be heart bruising. However, it is emotionally and psychologically healthier to relate with others appropriately and with a degree of flexibility.

Our relationships may converge, and then diverge, and converge again; defining a relationship is not binding and is of its moment in time. This helps us relate and also to be aware of the direction of closeness; if we are becoming more distant with someone and we wish to be closer, being aware of the change can enable us to open a discussion and perhaps converge towards closeness again.

The spectrum of the human condition is very broad and the dynamical range of early home unconscious conditioning will reflect this; from those with safe loving homes who now have an unconscious need to replicate conditions or warmth and security to those who experience forms of brutality in their formative years and may take a whole lifetime to grow through the healings of such deep wounds. One of the types of impact from deep early wounding will be covered in a later chapter; When Love = pain.

Often, the early home holds a blend of different emotions and the combinations can sometimes be challenging to handle and also send mixed messages to the world.

If awareness is the first step towards change, then understanding is the first step towards acceptance. Being aware of one's own unconscious and emotional needs can be very helpful in the art of relating. Being aware of a partner's, or prospective partner's dynamics can make navigating the waters of human relating less turbulent.

Romance and Commitment.

For clarity, I am going to address these two realms of relating in the same section because it is easier to consider them in contrast with one another. However, they are distinctly different from one another. It is possible to have lots of romance with someone - but no commitment. It is also possible to have commitment from someone - and the relationship is rather short on romance.

In a sense, commitment is the outgrowth of romance. If we are crass for a moment, one could think of romance and dating as the dance of seduction and capture, and then commitment as the greater task of ensuring love's longevity.

Our psychological and emotional, philosophical and ideological approach to Romance may be completely different to how we consider Commitment. For some people the two things are similar and for others they are virtually the same.

Romance may hold the thrill of the chase, the tingle of 'not knowing', the excitement of discovery, of converging, of falling deeper and deeper into love. It can be breathless and beautiful.

Commitment can be rewarding on a level that romance can only dream of. Two Souls sharing time, making memories, making a home in a perfect blend of the best of both of their acquired tastes. When the balance and harmony are in-tune, and the alchemy is mutually enriching, life in a committed relationship which suits us can bring incredible happiness.

Occasionally, what might seem a natural transition from romance into a deeper commitment can go awry. There are instances of couples who have lived together for many years choosing to get married and then separating and divorcing within a year. To many, this is puzzling; the couple have a track record of getting on well, they may have started a family together, in fact, they get on so well that they have decided to step into legal or spiritual ritualistic commitment. What has gone wrong?

Sometimes the transition from one context of relating to another; in this case, from continuous-courtship to witnessed-commitment, can also trigger for one, or both, partners a transition in identity. It may be the case that for one, or both, partners, the act of 'stepping over the line', into commitment or marriage or hand-fasting send a signal to a dormant archetype slumbering within their unconscious that it now time to awaken and become salient. How life is viewed, how life is heard, how they express themselves, their opinion of who they are may now be 'filtered' through a lens of; 'this is how I am supposed to be', or, this is how things are supposed to be'. If our relationship with a facet of life changes then we change in how we interrelate with it. Years of living together is a certain context worked very well. The context was changed in the unconscious of one, or both, partners and so the dynamics of the relationship itself reflected the new paradigm. Getting married or hand-fasted doesn't always prompt a divergence, of course, it can also prompt a convergence and closer loving partnership. The type of change I am describing here seems to occur in couples who have previously lived together for many years, and, of course, it is dependent upon the quality or condition of the 'sleeping archetypes'.

Another challenging dynamic that appears to walk arm in arm with love is that of self-worth and an anticipation of rejection.

Self worth is an important part of love in life. We can only share that which we possess, so if we have a love for ourselves in our hearts, and I mean a healthy self-love, then we have love to share. Also, when we know we are worthy of love we are more open to receiving love from others. This may all sound rather obvious, and I sincerely hope that it does, because there are people for whom accepting and sharing love is challenging, and accepting anything of value from life is a path rarely travelled.

When I was 32 and just embarking on my life changing training in Neuro-Holistic Therapy; an eclectic blend of Hypnotherapy, NLP and Psychobiology, my teacher Michael Harrison asked me a peculiar question. We were discussing success and my inability to get work flowing through my life. I held the view that success was, 'something out there', like an intangible mysterious quality or secret knowledge that others had and I was excluded from. Michael listened quietly for a moment and simply asked; 'When are you going to give up poverty?'.

An amazing light-bulb moment - a revelation !

It wasn't that success was out of my arm's reach at all; it was that I was successfully maintaining my poverty. My attitude, sense of focus; the words I used to describe myself, my learned habits of seeing myself as small and ineffective - all of these were the inner components which created by responses and reactions to people, which in turn closed doors in life. Changing my relationship towards myself changed how I related to the world and doors began to open that I would have thought impossible just a few years before.

The things I learned from Michael were part of a course of training which I took over in 1994 and have been teaching ever since. I love showing other people how they can open doors to new pathways.
An example of higher self-worth working:

One afternoon, I had a phone call from 'Amethyst'. She told me she had a job interview the following day, her voice betraying an unusually high level of anxiety; it was a very important day. Being a single parent it was hard for her to find work that had flexible within their hours of working that would accommodate the school run and allow her to be home for the kids after work.

For a number of years Amethyst had stayed in the same administration job, despite the fact there were no opportunities for growth. She didn't get on with her boss that well and, being a very small firm, the atmosphere was important to her.

So, there she was the day before her interview for a job that was just perfect and Amethyst was very nervous. After we had talked about work for a while I asked about the rest of her life and how things were generally. Her love life wasn't quite right and she wanted to move from the house she was in and also the area she lived in. To me it seemed there was an underlying issue happening here: Amethyst had unconsciously, quite unwittingly, 'set up' most of the areas of her life in ways that were unsatisfactory, and this seemed to be the key.

It turned out that Amethyst had a small image of her Self, a pessimistic internal voice, and 'fight or flight' breathing patterns around the notions of success, reward, wealth and being judged; mainly because she was already judging herself and her judgement, her unconscious conclusion, was that she was 'not good enough' *and* 'didn't deserve it', *and,* 'it'll all go wrong I just know it'.

These notions and attitudes produced a set of emotions which triggered a set of physiological conditions which in turn led her into consciously, and unconsciously, making decisions that caused the failures and problems to come about. This was done through:

- Using 'downbeat' voice tones.

- Not taking opportunities because of an expectation of it being a waste of time.

- Assuming the worst – or at least a mediocre result.

- and more besides ... I'm sure you get the picture

I guided Amethyst through a series of Neuro-Holistic Therapy exercises that would improve her internal pictures of herself, change what she automatically told herself about being Amethyst, and we performed an exercise to connect slower and deeper breathing to the idea of being in any interview or judgement situation.

After the session, Amethyst found that whenever she thought about herself, she saw herself as being big in size, about 15 feet tall, surrounded with bright light and the sound of joyful dancing music that seemed to radiate out from within her. Because her breathing controlled her calmness/anxiety levels, I helped Amethyst find an easy way to deliberately breathe slowly while concentrating on a conversation – and her whole manner became more cheerful and brighter.

She got the job. In fact, after the first interview she was called that same afternoon asking her to please come right away for the second interview. They had cancelled the interviews with the other candidates. Amethyst still enjoys her job, and she also met her current partner there. They have a wonderful relationship and Amethyst's friends are secretly 'window-shopping for hats'. All these issues and changes were connected to Amethyst's sense of self-worth and value. When she became valuable to herself, others found themselves in agreement with her conclusions. Her judgement is now, '*I am fantastic!*'

In a job interview …

A person with a rich sense of inner worth will find your unconscious communicating success through the appropriate body language, voice tones, general attitude, aura and subjective experience that creates the environment within which it is easy and natural for an interviewer to be in good rapport and suitably impressed. An enriched inner worth brings about the expectation of success – and your life measures up to it.

A person with an impoverished sense of inner worth could find themselves in the opposite type of situation. Their internal state of 'being unworthy' is often communicated unconsciously and encourages the external world to intuitively respond accordingly. This then adds to the 'evidence' of unworthiness, and the internal impoverished image becomes even stronger.

Years of either these rich, or impoverished, dynamics being re-enforced obviously leads to different sets of people being convinced that no matter what they do (conscious decision making) they are 'stuck' with 'their lot' (unconscious self image).

A host of questions now surface, such as:

- Is all this true?

- Can your lot be changed?

It changed for Amethyst, so therefore it can change for you.

What would happen if your unconscious now began to update your internal image and sense of self-worth while you are now reading these very words ?

If your unconscious now began to choose to change right now, or perhaps later in a day dream or while you sleep at night, or even perhaps just at the unconscious level, to create for itself an enriching sense of self- worth and self-image. What would happen in your life after your unconscious has already completed the entire process of enriching your value in such a way you just find yourself making decisions, and unconsciously behaving in ways, without any effort, that encourage more and more success in your life – on every level. So you find your taste for food just naturally leads you to choosing the healthy option; because it's what you really want. You find yourself making space in your life to relax, peacefully relax. You find the idea of reading, studying, learning and broadening your depth of knowledge makes you buzz and just becomes fun to do. You find your ability to relate to others becomes easier as you become fascinated by their viewpoints and ways of looking at life. Stepping into another's world is just a natural part of building empathy and rapport and encourages people to warm to you more and more often. This creates an energy around you that draws success towards you find you only want to do things that enhance the overall quality of your life, building more harmony for you and those you love. What would it be like to find yourself naturally thinking of creative and practical ways to improve your financial and career position that brought an enriched long-term effect on your life, your family and the world around you. If, after your unconscious now completes the process you have an increased value for the environment within which you live your life, what would change in your behaviour?

- What would change in your attitude?

- What would change in your beliefs about what is possible for you?

- What would it be like to be the enriched you now?

Whatever you may clearly, or vaguely, or unconsciously have just wondered, it would be the case that having just considered those answers caused you to imagine, or picture, or feel or say things to yourself which were different to your old ways; more uplifting and optimistic. With this in mind, the chemicals in your body changed, even if only slightly. Your breathing and heart rate changed along with your enjoyment of 'what it is to be you'. This also created a change in your overall energy field – and this has already changed what you are drawing towards you right now.

It is good to remember that sometimes change is a process as well as an event. Drawing things towards you that are only a short step away will bring about events that happen very quickly. Drawing things towards you that are further away may entail the initial process of completing of the first step ... before you take the second step that leads to the goal of an enriched life for you.

'What we are now ... attracts ... what we are now'.

You've probably noticed in nature that like attracts like. I've never seen a humming bird mate with a duck and hippos don't hang around with giraffes. We are no different. 'Rock 'n' rollers' wouldn't be seen dead with the 'classicals' and the classicals wouldn't be seen dead with the rock 'n' rollers. Likewise, the uglies aren't seen with the beautiful ones and the beautiful ones wouldn't be seen dead with the uglies.

' Opposites attract within the same type'

In order to determine who we are going to associate with and what kinds of people we will magnetically gravitate towards, we have to first either consciously, or unconsciously, label ourselves. This labelling process can be spread out over the entire developmental period of around seven to fourteen with each experience that we have during this time going into the pot and colouring our self perception. Some of the experiences for some people may not be easy to deal with.

The experience of low self esteem brought into play in the formative years between 7 and 14, and their impact on loving relationships later in life:

<u>Jade:</u>

As a young person, around the ages of ten to fourteen, Jade's social skills were 'stifled' by her strict parents. During this time Jade had experiences that enabled her to form the conclusion that in some way playing is either not allowed, frowned upon, or only to be considered 'when all work is done and finished'. For her this meant there was at best a restricted playing time, and at worst no playing time at all. Jade also felt her friends were severely scrutinised, or so it seemed, by her restrictive parents: all these factors made it difficult to make friends and she began to avoid the whole issue altogether; finding herself isolated and lonely as a result. The ramifications of these kinds of experiences led to notions of expected rejection based on the now in-built identity of being a person that is in some way 'unacceptable'.

If we see ourselves as unacceptable, then it is perfectly natural to assume others will find us unacceptable too. 'Why should I bother to approach people if, "it's all going to go wrong anyway ?'

When Jade did manage to reach out to people and begin relating to them she found herself in relationships which were unsatisfactory. The part of her mind that had a poor self-image would only allow Jade to behave in an approachable way if the person was somehow unacceptable to her. If she found herself really liking someone, she automatically assumed they would find her to be not good enough. Armed and primed with expectations of rejection she managed to avoid rejection from people she really liked by associating with people she only 'sort of liked'. This meant she would not be rejected by people she really liked – and it worked. However, as a strategy for getting close to really nice people, it was wildly counter-productive. Many years of re-enforcing these notions led Jade to wholeheartedly believe she was unacceptable, and not worth a second look.

On this basis, any compliment that was paid to Jade became something to be treated with suspicion, because the very idea that 'Jade is good looking' is obviously a lie. It's obviously a lie because it does not fit Jade's pre-judged model of the world, of her 'rejection-reality' which is coloured by her (most often unconscious) internal self-image. If, and it is a big maybe if, the complimentor is actually telling the truth of their, 'clearly illusory', opinion, then Jade, with her impoverished self- image, has to now make sure that the truth really is being told. It is hard to trust a compliment when you believe it does not fit; and harder still to trust the person who has expressed it without *changing something within onself*. There are many pathways to changing oneself but Jade was unaware that effective talking therapies like Neuro-Holistic Therapy even existed. She was 'stuck', and Jade would unconsciously push nice people away.

So, now her tests begin. Our heroic complimentor might be asked, 'Do you really think I am pretty?', and he steps onto the wobbly path of attempting to convince a heart-bruised person that they are in fact, wonderful. A few nice words may not be enough. Regular flowers and a poem and a song might not be enough either. Jade's complimentor may have to swim the lake of crocodiles, fight the wild ninjas, run through the wall of fire, climb the broken-glass covered tower, reach his beautiful maiden and *then* has to help Jade to recover her self esteem because otherwise the scene goes like this:

'Ok, you are worthy of me, but, *am I* worthy of you?'

In the core of the bruised self esteem can lay a deeper fear. The fear of success, or 'being seen', of responsibility and of trusting oneself to make the 'right' decision. Such fears appear to have the perspective that when one sets one's feet onto a path in life, that one is somehow stuck with is, as if doomed to walk one's fate. Of course, we know this isn't the case, but for some people, sometimes, it can feel like it. It is possible for a person to hold, for example, their promise in a marriage vow in an esteem that is higher than their own physical safety. To approach commitment as if it is a choice one can never change or undo would make the pressure of, 'getting it right', so intense that it could have an immobilising effect and the person is unable to overcome the fear of becoming 'eternally involved'.

Obviously, these are very deep issues and if you, or someone you know, is experiencing such things then I would highly recommend that professional effective help is sought; it can be very rewarding.

After a few consultations, progressively working on the image of herself that was stored in her unconscious, Jade became open, expressive and adventurous in the quest to joyfully embrace what she truly wanted in life.

It was the bruised condition of Jade's own worthiness that created her relating problems. What purpose might this serve a Soul learning here in Earth school? Well, in a spiritual sense, this allows the karmic waves of fortune to wash ashore a person who has the stamina, skill, courage, ability, and a deep enough love to *want* to turn around Jade's capacity for self and other love. Once done, the rewards are astounding. Ask anyone who has a kind of secret smile and a partner with an old fearful notion of 'automatic rejection' they have overcome, and you'll know why Jade's partner considers himself to be a lucky man.

Intimacy

A profound dynamics of human relating is intimacy. Intimacy can mean different things, intimacy can share many experiences. Let's try and define it.

Intimacy describes the experience of sharing of the self. Intimacy is a quality of depth; not a relationship to narrative, expectation, of proximity or of time.

It is possible to experience intimacy with a person whom we never even meet. For example, you could be on a river-ferry crossing one afternoon and from the other side of the boat you catch a stranger's eye. They burn into your very soul and, although you never spoke or discovered their name, those beautiful eyes haunt you for years and years. On the other hand, you can sit next to someone on the bus going to work for 20 years and never really know or 'see' the person in all that time.

It is possible to share your house with someone, your breakfast table, your bed and even your body; but still not share your deepest heart.

The Elizabethans used to call the orgasm, 'The little death'; because, when two people share an orgasm together, 'I' dies and 'we' is born.

For some people, opening up on such a deep level is a frightening prospect whilst for others it is life's greatest joy. Whatever our relationship with intimacy, it holds a special place at the heart of human relating.

In many cultures, a marriage is not considered to be complete until it is consummated. The hats and dresses and finely dressed men, the altar and the flowers, are the enactment of ritual, of ceremony, of the idea of relating during which the narrative of identity is changed. The stuff of deep connecting though, comes in the bridal suite after the public ceremony is done. This is where the two souls mingle and exchange not just glances and words, touch and gesture, but the waters within which a new, incoming life may flow.

From a zen and tantra perspective, this is a deeply spiritual experience. Esotericists suggest that not only do we entwine physically, but we also entwine etherally through our aura and astrally too; in its beauty it is a joining of two souls sharing one light.

However, the feelings evoked here are very powerful and they may become entangled with other concerns. When we expose ourselves to such deep emotions we may also experience feelings arising from the unconscious which have been subdued or repressed, sometimes for many years. There is a powerful surge when repressed material becomes conscious again, and the powerful surge of love making can sometimes trigger the release of powerful feelings back into conscious awareness again.

This means that getting closer to another person may also facilitate our getting closer to ourselves. Again, this may be welcoming and joyous, or frightening and to be avoided at all costs, depending on your perspective and situation in life.

I cannot recommend highly enough that one seeks a path of self discovery and of resolving one's deeper issues stored within your unconscious. To attempt to do this by oneself can also be emotionally bruising and I would always advocate that you find a competent, skilled professional to be your guide. Please always go psychologically deep-sea diving with a guide.

Your unconscious wants to release old unfinished material to be resolved and released from the system. This does not mean we have to embrace our history with loving arms, but we can learn to accept having survived our past and, hopefully, find something fruitful within whatever we have experienced which will enable us to grow with wisdom and a greater sense of self enlightenment.

Voluntarily looking for issues to resolve in a safe environment such as a consulting room is an expedient and easier way. An alternative is for your unconscious to steer your thoughts, narratives, words, gestures, reactions, decisions and behaviours in such a manner that you find yourself in circumstances which seem to reflect, if not replicate, the original circumstance of the feelings which were repressed and not dealt with.

Our ancestors evolved this very important part of our psychological protective system and it is highly efficient.

If we find ourselves feeling very embarrassed while a teacher and our classmates laugh at our mistake while reading out loud, the emotion may be too much to handle in that moment and the feelings are ushered into an 'amnesia box' and remain there, impatiently waiting for an opportunity to express themselves so they can then leave the system and we can be free from their background anxiety. If we do not create a circumstance in which they can find expression, during a psychological consultation or even during an in-depth astrology reading (anything which illuminates the deeper self), your unconscious will navigate your feet into finding yourself being called upon to make a spontaneous presentation before the important delegation; completely unplanned and with no foreknowledge of what is written on the Powerpoint slides you are going to present in front of your boss and work colleagues. Your unconscious seizes the chance and induces a tiny little moment of dyslexia; the wording became blurred in the overly-warm heat of the moment and a simple word is mispronounced and the feelings of acute embarrassment radiate from flushed cheeks and shuffling feet, finally leaving the system after all those years.

These mechanisms are at play when we play with one another in intimate moments. It is no wonder that relationships can take us into the brightest light or the deepest shadow.

Sometimes, we exhibit patterns of behaviour, in relationships or work or hobbies or adventures, which seem to take us around the same old path. We can have so many similar types of experience with a certain relationship dynamic 'happening again', that it can feel as if we are stuck on a page or fated to experience this repeating thing.

We may feel fated, but are we creatures of free will or are we like puppets, merely acting out the script of some higher organising power?

How are we to make such a judgement about the nature of life and being human?

Loyalty, Happiness and Self Expression

Personal Power, Depression and the Light of Your Inner Flame

Loyalty is a very important thing for me; but, loyalty to whom?

Or perhaps, loyalty to what?

Politically, I am not partisan; I have never been a member of any political party and I am very much a champion of social justice, fairness and compassion. When it comes to personal relationships; friendships, students, chums, loved ones, girlfriends, I have come to realise that I have a deep and enduring loyalty to happiness :)

The feeling of happiness, in my world, is not a constant sensation. It rises and falls, like an undulating wave. To me, happiness is like this:

If someone views happiness as a destination, as an object, like something to acquire or hold, they may find it is rather like holding a vague mist.

Happiness it seems, is not something which we find within objects either; when we acquire something, or achieve something, we experience a momentary sense of delight, of victory and even sometimes validation, but these are not a sense of happiness. They feel good, of course they do, but happiness is more than a passing sensation of feeling good.

To me, it seems happiness is an undulating emotion which emerges from a number of combining factors; it is more an orientation, rather than a destination. Among these are a sense of purpose in what we are doing at any given time, and a sense that what we have already done is somehow bearing fruit or 'working' for us. An optimism about future conditions is a part of it and a sense of self-acceptance sits at the core of it. It also seems important that we feel accepted by our society; and I don't mean, 'society', but rather the society that we admire at any particular moment; whether that is one person, a club, a gang, a culture, an ideology, a guild ...

Glee, delight, victory, reward, external-validation, external-approval, a round of applause, the words, 'I love you', all of these are transitory and flow though the moments of our lives like a precious nectar of the heart. Happiness, to me, is the light of the soul, a deeper smile that lives in the heart of your feelings. It is born from a general disposition towards kindness; for the self, and for all life forms with which we each make contact.

This post is, of course, not a statement of truth; it is just how things seem to me, an opinion of a Dave. I may not be the brightest filament in the bulb, so I go with the wording of a very intelligent man as a working guide:

'A human being is part of the whole, called by us 'universe,' a part limited in time and space. He experiences himself, his thoughts and feelings, as something separate from the rest -- a kind of optical delusion of consciousness. This delusion is a kind of prison for us, restricting us to our personal desires and to affection for a few persons nearest to us. Our task must be to free ourselves from this prison by widening our circle of compassion to embrace all living creatures and the whole of nature in its beauty. Nobody is able to achieve this completely, but the striving for such achievement is in itself part of the liberation, and a foundation for inner security':

Albert Einstein

I once described wisdom as the culmination of the Soul's learning which orientates the heart towards choosing and responding instinctively, on the pre-conscious level, with kindness and compassion as an innate sense of self. I have come to the current realisation that my loyalty is towards feeling happiness in my heart. I am not blindly loyal to ideas, concepts, philosophies, political parties, musical genres or people.

If an idea, a concept, a philosophy or political policy lights up my heart, I shall champion it and promote it, and emotionally be drawn towards it. If an idea, a concept, a philosophy or political policy makes my heart frown, I shall become emotionally disconnected from it, and my feet will create an increasing distance from it.

Likewise, if interacting with a person lights up my heart, I am emotionally drawn towards them and seek to interact more deeply, behaving in ways which encourage more interactions to happen as often as possible.

If interacting with a person makes my heart frown, I become emotionally disconnected and my feet create an increasing distance from that person; conversationally, emotionally and physically, and, if my heart frowns with enough sadness, I disconnect completely.

Like a clam opening and closing, becoming close or distant, my feet follow my heart and it happens quite unconsciously, below the threshold of my awareness. This is not personal, and as my ongoing interactions with people occur, the sensations of happiness are constantly assessed and my sense of distance or closeness reflects this;

My heart opens when I feel relaxed, secure and safe :)

My heart closes when I feel vulnerable, uncertain or frightened :(

Kindness, compassion, politeness, courtesy, gentleness, curiosity and a willingness to learn and explore life and this realm with humour, wit, intelligence and elegance are like bright lanterns to the eye of my attention. It is like a very simple equation:

Pleasant stuff = being proximate induces a smile in my heart; out of loyalty to my happiness I seek to maintain proximity .

Unpleasant stuff = being proximate induces unhappiness in my heart; out of loyalty to my happiness I seek to create and maintain distance.

I am loyal to that which is nutrient and good for me and disloyal to that which is toxic and detrimental for me. This is an act of self care and Hermetic in nature; 'As above then so below'. My heart and mind, as well as my body, have a well functioning and fastidious immune system.

I can think of nothing more wonderful than sharing time in wonderful company ; sharing life and time here with you. Sharing time in the company of someone with whom my heart glows with joy is one of the most beautiful expressions of life that time can bring.

All forms of life seek to express themselves; daffodils flood Britain with yellow in the spring, zebras do their stripy thing and horse chestnut trees yield a conker or two. It is natural for everything in nature to express its form of life. That is, it seems, except with some humans. In human relating, we can either express ourselves, or depress ourselves.

Human expression can take two basic forms; anger or assertion. Anger can be defined as a form of expression which destroys things while assertion can be defined as a form of expression which builds things. Sometimes, the distinction between the two is not very clear.

If we are not expressing ourselves then we may turn the eye of our attention inwards and depress ourselves. Frustration, irritation, annoyance, being miffed, anger, rage and finally lethargy and an absence of ability to express oneself or even move; a complete sense of depression. The dynamical range of depression is just as varied and broad as that of expression, though hidden and beneath the surface. These dynamical ranges are not static and we may pass through them in varying periods of time; from a fleeing moment of irritation to years entrapped in immobilising depression. We may bounce manically like a cork through the entire rainbow, from the despair of immobilisation through to an expressive creativity which illuminates and excites the world.

The feeling of this, the spirit of the inner flame which seeks expression has a variety of names; Chi and Ki from eastern esoteric philosophy, Mars from astrology, energy or spirit from Western esoteric philosophy, arousal and affect from neuroscience.

I would like to take a moment to define 'Affect', in the way that it is used as a noun in Affective Neuroscience.

Affective Neuroscience is an emerging discipline, exploring the neurobiology of emotions. Jaak Panksepp, a key figure and pioneer in Affective Neuroscience, suggests that a neurological understanding of the basic operations of the mammalian brain may provide a unifying understanding between different approaches to the human condition and psychology; such as ethology, behaviourism and the cognitive sciences.

A tenet of affective neuroscience is the role that emotions and subjective experience play in the causal chain of events which control action, and these arise from neurobiological events which regulate and modulate instincts and experience. This approach contrasts the materialistic view that mind and body are distinct and different and that there is a mini self within the self; a homunculus which perceives sensory afferent data, such as visual signals, as if on a mini screen within the mind, like watching a screen in a theatre. Antonio Domasio has described what is known as the 'dualism of the Cartesian theatre' as, 'Descarte's error,' suggesting that mind and body share a relationship from which subjective experience emerges. Neuroscience has recently begun to direct its attention away from anatomy-as-causality towards a systems orientated approach between body and brain.

Affect is a term borrowed from German psychology and describes an independent pattern of sensory input which forms the pre-conscious basis of the experience of emotion before it is distilled into a cognitive awareness of feeling; in other words, it is the arousal or energy that moves through our system before an emotion emerges.

Panksepp suggests that emotional abilities initially emerge from instinctual operating systems of the brain, which allow animals to begin gathering food, information and other resources needed to sustain life. Emotive systems undergo refinement in higher brain areas as they mature and organisms make effective behavioural choices. Emotional tendencies such as those related to fear, anger and separation-distress emerge during early developmental stages, providing coping strategies for dealing with emergencies which might compromise survival. Other emotional systems such as seeking, play, nurturance and sexuality have a role in establishing and maintaining social structures which may in turn influence propagation. Primary affective states may have evolved to facilitate rapid adaptive responses to phenomena by learned association and emotional arousal which form a gestalt mood to prompt specific behaviour. In *Affective Consciousness*, Panksepp writes;

At minimum, affective consciousness can be parsed into at least three general varieties:

(i) the exteroceptively driven sensory-affects that reflect the pleasures and aversions of worldly objects and events.

(ii) the interoceptively driven homeostatic-affects, such as hunger and thirst, that reflect the states of the peripheral body along the continuum of survival.

(iii) the emotional-affects that reflect the arousal of brain instinctual action systems that are built into sub-neocortical regions of the brain as basic tools for living – to respond to major life challenges such as various life-threatening stimuli (leading to fear, anger, and separation-distress) and the search for various life-supporting stimuli and interactions (reflected in species-typical seeking and playfulness, as well as socio-sexual eagerness and maternal care).

In the field of psychology there are, however, two different meanings given to the term; *Affect*.

Classical psychoanalysis and attachment theory view affects in distinctly different ways.

Classical psychoanalysis approaches affects as a unitary phenomenon of drives and primitive powerful forces, which may be categorised as positive or negative, both of which may be considered to be of value in certain contexts.

In contrast, attachment theorists' approach affects from a systems perspective, viewing the interrelation of affects as a heterogeneous process of regulation. This approach also encapsulates the psycho-social perspective of viewing the individual as a situated part of a relational whole. Affect regulation is an embodied system which functions in a similar way to the homeostasis, arousing or deactivating affects in response to experience.

There is a growing voice within the psychotherapeutic world since the end of the 20th century of how Affective Neuroscience and Interpersonal Neurobiology can assist not only in self understanding but also in enhancing therapeutic approaches to healing and transformation.

Authors such as Panksepp, Schore, Domasio, Cozolino, Seigal and others suggest that because we are biologically creatures of a system of chemistry which is constantly seeking to be in equilibrium, along with homeostasis, our system is in a state of flux in a quest to regulate our Affect. In other words, our moods change and shuffle about in a quest to find feelings of ease.

It is proposed that all psychpathological dispositions, from depression to obsessive compulsive disorder to bi-polar and dissociative disorders, have their roots in Affect Dysregulation. Guiding a person into being able to self-regulate their Affect in safe, productive and purposeful ways may be considered to be the core aim of therapeutic intervention. This model forms the bedrock of Neuro-Holistic Therapy.

It must be noted that there are many types of depression and the type I am discussing here in this chapter is the type in which a person feels their sense of expression is being thwarted. There are depressions of despair, of deep pessimism and the sense 'that all things will come to a bad end'. There are types of depression that are haunting and forlorn, like a kind of 'diving homesickness'. People experience depression in different ways and it seems to be the case that finding some form of expression is emotionally, psychologically and physiologically healthy. To find a way of expression whatever we are expressing in a way that is also life enhancing and of service to the world can appeal to our need for altruistic social inclusion and we have within us an emotion which is best described as; 'feeling good'

To borrow the term for Affect from Astrology for a moment of Mythos ...

Mars has two Moons orbiting around it. The Greeks called the Moons of Mars Phobos and Deimos, meaning fear and flight. The Romans held a different view of Mars. The root of this name, *Mar*, means origination, to grow, to shine and can be found within many names meaning 'mother'. Sasportas writes; 'this time he is accompanied by his squires Honus (Honour) and Virtus (Virtue).

When we express ourselves honestly, or how some might term 'authentically' or 'congruently', it feesl good. We each have a rightful place in the symphony of creation and giving expression to our unique niche of experience is to give honour to our part in creation.

On Judgement and Beauty

When I was 18, I read a number of quotes that made a deep impression:

One was; 'The only way round a problem is ... through it'.

Another; 'To be a gentleman one must be a truly gentle man'.

And another that caught my eye:

'Love and scandal are the best sweeteners of tea'.

Many spiritual teachings, in both embodied teaching and in book form, suggest that spiritual progress can only be made if an individual stops being judgmental. For ordinary human nature though, this is virtually impossible.

We have to make judgements on phenomena we encounter - it is how we navigate our way through the world. If we fail to judge the speed and direction of a bus we may be crushed if we step in front of it. If we fail to judge correctly the suitability, or not, of individual's character when combined with our own, the resultant mess, disappointment or anger may cause a great deal of discomfort for others that we care for, as well as for ourselves.

However, to pre-judge; to be prejudiced and make an assessment prior to investigation, is where many of the problems in personal and social dynamics reside.

Prejudice, in my opinion, is the ugly face of mankind.

It is very difficult to step out of a cultural habit of making pre-judgments and forming opinions of others before one has a full grasp of all of the facts available; and yet, if we are to grow in understanding we must endeavour to make this orientation the tone of our path. I have observed, over the years, my astrology students grow in confidence as they step out of the habit of forming opinions about people, such as awkward, good, bad, right, wrong, nice, unpleasant, etc and instead step into the light of being able to describe what they find without attaching a personal opinion to it.

When a person forms an opinion of another person, or circumstance, there is a possibility that the opinion may be incorrect if it is formed from a position of having missing information; any information. If you meet an adult who is unable to construct sentences coherently one might decide that the person is stupid, until one learns they have dyslexia and then, suddenly, the incoherence is explained and becomes perfectly natural; now we may possibly have a bright person who needs to be given a little more time and space in conversation and, thankfully, when the dyslexia is known about, people often do give them enough consideration.

So, if we have enough insight into a person's background, a deep enough understanding of their history, their drives, their dreams, hopes, fears , we can empathically walk in their shoes and it becomes harder to merely condemn them.

Are we able then to perceive life's gossips and opinion formers as clumsy linguists, who for some reason are either unable, or unwilling, to look deeply at life and human nature and enter the realm of wisdom and understanding. It might be possible that some souls choose such a path in order for those with an aptitude for wisdom and insight to become prompted to develop it within themselves.

What can we learn from the crass and uncouth, the shallow and the prejudgemental ?

What did we learn about ourselves from our condemnation of the rather dyslexic G W Bush?

Can we have a bright Obama without first having a dull George to contrast against?

There are, currently, in excess of 7 billion people on planet Earth, all with their own fingerprints, DNA, and their own personal perspective of life; their own unique lens on reality. The nature of life, truth, and the universe, as seen from precisely their place, in each unique moment of time, is utterly unique to them. Perhaps the truth can only be known fully by blending together the sum total of all human truths; but even then, it still won't be a full picture of reality; The Truth!

A fox can hear a beetle walk across a carpet - I can't. A shark can easily detect the electrical field of other creatures - I can't. There are realms of perception, like a dog's hearing, that are way beyond my scope of comprehension. So, like frequencies on a radio's spectrum of stations, my consciousness can only tune in to the human stations, and then it seems to often be somehow stuck on frequency 'Dave'.

I find astrology is a good vehicle for enabling me to gain a glimmer of other lenses of perception outside of my own. Some of them so far removed from what seems to be my natural view of understanding that they seem odd, or strange at first. That first encounter with another's perception of life that is different to our own is often called by people, 'odd', 'strange' or 'weird'. Later, when we are used to the notion that other's realities are just as valid as our own, we may find ourselves calling them 'interesting', or 'cool', or 'amazing'.

Perhaps people who call others odd, or strange, are just at the 'first glance' stage of experiencing realities other than their own and they need encouragement and friendly guidance; just as more experienced souls may once have done.

Linguistically, NLP tells us that humans tend to delete, distort and generalise information, especially in casual and informal conversation. It would take too much effort and time to explicitly relate all of the detail of our experiences, all of the time. And yet, as we may already know; if we leave details out we may invite the possibility of error. When we shorten sentences for expedience we may run the risk of misinforming or of being misleading.

For example, if someone says, 'Your jacket looks silly', the recipient may hear the words as if they are an authoritative statement of fact; the voice of the universe, or deity, or God has spoken, (read in a deep booming voice;); 'The jacket is Silly!'

However, the actual truth is that the sentence was not uttered by a god or a goddess or anything such like it; it was spoken by a human being, just another person among the other 7 + billion on the planet.

In essence then, this means that the weight, or magnitude, of the words, 'the jacket is silly', is not The Voice of Truth, but it is merely 1/7 billionth of the truth. Such a tiny small fraction of the actual reality. In fact, including this fact; for it is a Dave opinion and nothing more, every opinion we cast is nothing more than one seven billionth of the truth (human-truth).

Seen like this, opinions become just like grains of sand; we can give them great weight in our hearts if we wish to; though we do not need to anymore. I sometimes advise people who are sensitive to criticism and take other's opinions to heart, to take an alternative approach instead:

The alternative strategy is to now, silently, in your own mind, add the words, 'in my opinion', onto the end of people's sentences when they cast an opinion or declare something as if it is true.

For example, imagine someone saying the following statements out loud to you and you privately, with your own inner voice, add on the words presented in brackets and hear it as if it is their voice saying it. Allow for a ten second gap between each example:

'Your jacket looks silly' (in my opinion ...)

'You are an idiot' (in my opinion ...)

'It will all go wrong, you'll see' (in my opinion ...)

'That song is awful' (in my opinion ...)

'You like that movie? – it's rubbish' (in my opinion ...)

'They are all mad' (in my opinion ....)

By playing with the idea of adding the words, 'in my opinion', onto the end of their sentences, privately in your own imagination, the weight of their sentence is diminished and becomes much less authoritative. If you have a play with this, let me know what you find; I'd be really interested.

Everyone forms opinions; and so they should if they are to continue their evolutionary line and ensure that they avoid the poisonous red berries or evade capture by the malicious invader.

Perhaps then it shouldn't really come as a surprise to us that people form opinions, or that some people are pre-disposed towards making pre-judgments.

Maybe what really needs attention is our response towards these things. If we are upset by the malicious gossip or the slanders of others, why …?

What is it about the temporary passing opinions of these people, among the 7 billion that we could possibly mix with, that at this time seems to important to us?

How often do we find that, like raindrops travelling down a window, we may converge towards people and sometimes people diverge away from us and drift out of our lives altogether. Most of the people we worry about today may only feature in our story for a short time anyway.

Our reputation, our standing among our chosen society is important , of course; no man is an island and the quote at the start of this ramble on love and scandal hits the mark for precisely that reason. It is important that we are included, accepted, admired even. To be accepted by oneself is possibly one of the cornerstones of social self-confidence. Others may hold this opinion, or that opinion, but you know the truth within your heart; and if you are happy with your choices and behaviours then the light of that will shine through any cloud of self doubt.

One of the great voices of social rebellion, Bob Dylan, once said, 'To live outside of the law you must be honest'.

A tenet of NLP is that the value of the individual is held constant, while it is only the value of their behaviour which may be questioned if one is interested in being a helpful assistant for the soul. In this sense, a 'naughty child' isn't bad child; they are a good child who did a bad thing. The value of the behaviour is questioned but the child who performed the behaviour is always valued. Adopting this frame will yield the highest propensity for growth, healing, change and transformation.

One of my teachers, Michael Harrison, used to have, at the corner of all his training material, the axiom; 'Be … because, you are'.

'Mirror, mirror'

'A young Spring-tender girl
Combed her joyous hair …

'You are very ugly', said the mirror

But,

On her young lips hung
a smile of dove secret loveliness
for, only that morning had not
the blind boy said,
'You are beautiful …'

from *Small Dreams of a Scorpion* by Spike Milligan.

It is commonplace; it seems, for people to have an idea of themselves which is different to how others see them. The fashion and cosmetics industries lay testament to how much attention we, as social creatures, place on looks, image and the need to enchant or captivate.

And yet, 'what is beauty … ?'

Sasportas suggests that the ability we have as very small children to enchant and captivate our protectors and guardians, serves as a mechanism to further our survival. If we are the ones who come to mind when food is being distributed, if we can catch the eye of the adult who has a sitting-place next to the warm protective fire, then perhaps we may increase our chances of survival.

How we go about this is varies from person to person and with greater or lesser degrees of success. Physical attraction is just one of many strategies we may employ to engage the attention of someone.

The media, with its necessity for rapid responses and communications, adopts a stereotyping reductionist approach in its communications. The media's may be to enlighten, entertain and inform, but often a desire to deliver a quick sound-bite message means that considered thought is passed over in favour of something which will produce an instant emotion. It often seems as if the media has an intention to be provocative.

Poets have been wrestling with the question, 'what is beauty?', since language began and it is far too complex and sophisticated to define; beauty finds power in mystery and yet the fashion industry attempts to impose a single vision of beauty so that it can mass-market products, which dissempowers and reduces beauty to an empty sense of momentary passing thrill; women are encouraged to feel inadequate in order to need to spend more to try to fit with a single view of beauty; a sequence of behaviours which would read like a recipe for anxiety and neurosis if you were to take a step back and look at it objectively.

A zebra doesn't feel guilty about having stripes, and neither should it; it does stripy-ness brilliantly, just as I do being me brilliantly, and you are great at being you ...

We change, we grow, we unfold and become; and in each moment there is no better way to express the beauty of our reality other than to simply be who we are. If you believe the universe has a power of creation at its heart, then to be yourself is to pay honour to creation; to mask or hide yourself is akin to saying, the powers of creation didn't do a good enough job...

Has mother nature really made an error?

Or, is the human mind so easily influenced by traditions, customs, cultures and media that people have become accustomed to assuming they are somehow imperfect when they are just naturally themselves?

We each have a choice when it comes to looking at our own beauty:

We can distort ourselves to fit into some kind of shape or look that other people have decided we 'should' or 'must' be...

or...

we can change how we look at the whole thing, find a sense of self-acceptance and relax...

In a previous chapter we explored the figure of speech, 'beauty is in the eye of the beholder', and found that whenever an individual passes comment on another person, it is not really a statement of truth about the person at all, but it is more a commentary on the ability for the person to perceive the beauty in another.

To say that an absolute beauty exists is a complete nonsense. In some parts of the world, slim people are favoured while in another part of the world a slim person would be instantly rejected. The Roman concept of beauty is quite different to a Victorian one or a modern magazine, so which beauty is the 'right' or 'correct' one?

None of them.

Beauty is subjective; which is great because we are all different. We are not machines, moulded and off-the-peg. There is no such thing as a standard-human. We are evolving organic beings, multicellular creatures in a multi-faceted society; we may be droplets in a big wave, but we each have our own unique place in it; along with our own DNA, our own finger prints - even our own astrological chart.

Sameness is not a human quality.

Difference is the thing that makes the difference; and so, it is our differences, our 'flaws' which make us attractive.

For all the things we do in life; great sports, great art, music, adventures, flying and dancing; behind and around it all are the dynamics of human relating. Relating is not easy...

A high quality of compatibility is a better goal we may aspire to and, in the process, we may encounter rejection.

Rejection is your friend!

Rejection is nature's way of removing from our sphere of experience that which does not truly suit us.

Our conscious minds might decide that we like a particular person for some reason, and this may become reframed into the language of 'should; this person 'should like me', or, that person is 'supposed to love me'. The language of 'should' reveals that a person has, often unconsciously, same kind of rule or yard stick or what constitutes 'normality' and that the person with the 'should rule' is comparing the world as they find it with an inaccurate expectation.

Deep within you, in the heart of your feelings, you know whether or not someone feels right. It always shows on your face. When we are in the company of someone who brings joy into our feelings it is virtually impossible to stop our face from bursting into a smile ... :)

When we are in the company of someone who, in this moment at least, does not resonate this way, our face shows an expression which is not a smile.

Sometimes we have to face it; being in someone's company may be a good idea, but is it a good feeling?

Love is best felt with the heart – leave ideas for the mind to wrestle with (it is very good at it)

Follow your feelings, listen you yourself and, if in doubt, give this simple technique a go:

Mirror Dowsing is a way of discerning what your heart feels about something if your mind is befuddled with unclear options. Generally, when our conscious mind is uncertain, it is because we can see different possibilities and pathways. What we instinctively feel is best may differ from what we want to be for the best. Also, an option or choice might clash with what we instinctively feel, while another choice may agree with what we instinctively feel. Mirror dowsing can help to clearly know what the heart feels and what we instinctively know is best for us at this time.

All emotions move through the body; we ripple with our feelings from moment to moment. Mostly, our changing emotions are so subtle and discrete that they are unconscious, meaning we are unaware of them. Dowsing is one way of being able to distinguish these emotive responses so they become observable.

The heart tends to reveal itself through the muscle movements in our face. The purpose of this exercise is to watch and observe the muscles reactions to a number of suggestions, and to refrain from doing any analysis or commentary until the entire exercise is complete.

Step one:

First of all, identify what you need clarity on, and describe it to yourself is a short clear sentence.. ie. Doing Dave's Online Astrology course.

Step two:

Sit comfortable in front of a mirror and relax a little ... allow your shoulders to relax ... let your hands settle and relax ... and slow your breathing a little; imagine you are placing your emotions into neutral...

Step three:

Now, think of an activity or circumstance which has nothing to do with what you wish to investigate. ie, say in your inner voice - 'drinking a glass of fruit juice' - and immediately watch what your face muscles *Do.*

Step four:

Watch the corners of your mouth;

do they rise, fall or remain the same?

what do your eye brows do?

Step five:

without giving a seconds thought to what this may, or may not mean, make a note of the response and immediately place your feelings in neutral again.

Step six:

Do this whole process about 6 more times, with a random list of unconnected things, some of which are pleasing and some of which are not; watching a falcon, seeing a favourite band, tidying a messy room, getting caught in a shower, meeting a good friend etc.

Step seven:

Then, when you have done more than 6, say the sentence which describes what you wish to find out about, in this example, ' Doing Dave's Online Astrology course', and watch to see what your face muscles Do.

NB:

If you want to ask more questions, spread them in between more random ones.

Once you have finished, look back at your responses to the suggestions or options and see what you find.

Which options of choices makes your face light up?

Beauty is a complex business and the art of relating, when our beauty mixes with another persons, is even more so. To me, it seems like relationships are alchemical; meaning not just a mix of chemistry, but a transformative experience as well - we are changed by those we are touched by. Sometimes, it is neither individual which is 'wrong' in a relationship, sometimes it is just a question of compatibilities; not so much the right or wrong person, but just a mis-fit:

Square pegs are great

Round holes are great

Square pegs in round holes are uncomfortable and taking the decision to diverge is sometimes the healthiest decision.

The converge-diverge-converge-diverge pattern may concertina quickly though an afternoon's changing moods or run over lifetimes; a life together, a life apart... an hour together, an hour apart...

Rather than judging oneself to be 'wrong' or unworthy or 'destined to be lonely', perhaps it is more a question of bumping into someone you like at a moment in time when it is fortuitous for that particular love to grow.

Sometimes, we may meet someone we like but there is an age difference - time problem

or, we may meet someone and there is a circumstance issue: space problem

If the bonds of mutual liking are strong enough, circumstances will rarely stop feet from finding one another, though sometimes it may be culturally politically dangerous; like crossing a gang, class, race or religious divide ...

The best approach is to have an open heart and an open mind and just enjoy life and meet people. Go to places where there is a higher chance you will meet the kind of person you wish to meet and increase your chances of bumping into someone who is compatible with you.

And, take good heart; there is absolutely nothing wrong with you - nothing at all

you are wonderful!

You are beautiful!!

We are beautiful!!!

Are we not...?

'av a word ...

Language, Relationships and the Narrative Self

During my childhood my local library had literally opened which enabled me to escape from a disadvantaged and impoverished start in life. I may now seem as if I am veering off at a tangent, but this will meander back to the theme of relating;

Stephen Fry is a very eloquent wordsmith, with a love of language; both old, traditional and modern. A few years ago he presented a fantastic documentary for the BBC on Johann Gutenberg, the inventor of the printing press. A couple of years later he drew upon what he had learned when researching the programme when he was asked to deliver an address before a youthful audience at the iTunes festival, held at the Roundhouse in London. He narrated the history of copyright, staring from the first written languages to the development of electronic recording equipment. Between these two points in history, stands Guttenberg's press; etched in time like a huge doorway that enabled the citizens of Earth, and I am not exaggerating, to become free, and to flourish in a celebration of their own innate identity.

Before the printing press, all books and texts were handwritten. What was written, the ability to write, the language of the writing, and the ability to read what was written was controlled by religion. If you were on the inside of the religion, you had access to the words endorsed by the authority. If you were outside of it – you were excluded. The advent of the printing press sent waves of change through societies. In a short space of time, hundreds of books were produced and knowledge, received in the same form in which it was recorded, was accessible to all.

There is a correlation between our character and how we meet circumstances in life. When faced with problems and challenges, we may stumble, or, we may thrive. There is a correlation between the architecture of our brain and our character. Stroke victims or those with degenerative brain diseases sometimes find that their character or style of personal expression is completely changed. If we lose our memories , then, who are we?

The architecture of the brain plays a vital role in affording the expression of the varying faces of who we are and who we may become. Our brain is the chalice which holds our alchemy.

Neuroscience has advanced leaps and bounds over the last decade and modern scanners reveal more about the relationship between brain and behaviour each year. Neural brain activity is accompanied by a narrative. This is an important point, and I'd like to paste an extract from one of my papers here ...

(This may get a little technical, but it's absolutely fascinating...)

The Narrative Self:

Stephen Pinker attests that humans have an instinct for language; 'Language is so tightly woven into human experience it is scarcely possible to imagine life without it' (Pinker, 1994). Words are not merely symbolic conveyers of ideas or meaning; the phenomena of language is a construct of what may be considered to be that which defines being human; a complex and sophisticated consciousness of self (Dennet, 1991). Consciousness does not appear to arise from any single region or neural network of the brain, but appears to be an emergent function which arises from the integration and synchrony of cycles of neural processing (Cozolino, 2002). In *The Feeling of What Happens*, Domasio describes the emergence of narrative as a process which begins with a proto-conscious core self:

> ...neural patterns which become images, images being the same fundamental currency in which the description of the consciousness-causing object is also carried out. Most importantly, the images that constitute this narrative are incorporated in the stream of thoughts. The images in the consciousness narrative flow like shadows along with the images of the object for which they are providing an unwitting, unsolicited comment. To come back to the metaphor of movie-in-the-brain, they are *within* the movie. There is no external spectator (Domasio, 1999).

Domasio asserts the autobiographical self is constituted by implicit memories of multiple instances of past experiences which grow continuously and may be partly remodelled to reflect new experiences. Sets of memories which describe identity and person can be reactivated as a neural pattern and made explicit as images (Domasio, 1999). Edelman and Tononi confer, describing the formation of the autobiographical self as, 'the remembered present', a higher-order of consciousness which can place itself in a scheme of the past, present and anticipated future, which, in its most developed form has a semantic and linguistic capability (Edelman and Tononi, 2000).

The architecture of the brain is not completely static and fixed. The term, 'Neuro Plasticity', is used to describe how the brain's shape is changed when different cells are used, a bit like making a new path in a field of soft tall grass. The more the path is used, the more ingrained the pathway becomes. If it falls out of use it can disappear. Yes; a whole chain of thought, an idea, can literally vanish from your head. American neuroscientists have coined the phrase, 'use it ... or lose it'.

So, the shape of our brain determines how easily we may, or may not, express facets of our character, including problem solving abilities and the options of thoughts we may have. Obviously, when faced with a challenge in life, the more choices we have through the soft long grass, the easier it may be to find a way to overcome the challenge and thrive.

Less thought options = less choices = higher chance of failure.

More choice options = more choices = higher chance of success ... and survival.

What creates the thought options?

Brain activity

What stimulates brain activity?

Our actions, the environment, and narrative; words.

What stimulates the brain with words while also providing us with new words, new thought choices, new pathways?

Books.

Books are a doorway into new possibilities in life. We can only reach the limit of our horizon; and we can expand our horizons by expanding our vocabulary; the more words we have at our disposal the more thought-choices we have at our neuro-finger tips.

The printing press didn't just remove knowledge from the clutches of religious control. It didn't just enable a reader to receive the precise wording, or thoughts, intended by the author. It didn't just enrich the vocabulary of ordinary men and expand their horizons of knowledge. It also, literally, fed and enriched the neuro-architecture of their brains.

The internet is a wonderful spreading words around the world in an instant. Note, I didn't say 'spreads knowledge', because sometimes the writing on the internet is inaccurate. Books can be inaccurate too, although they are often peer-reviewed in the sciences, they can deceive us and support all kinds of agendas. Books are also something we connect with, they touch us in a way that an electronic screen cannot seem to do so. For many people, books become their friends and can evoke a sentiment just as enriching as favoured music or art.

To have a moment or two browsing the shelves of a book shop is like stepping into a place where you can see, at a glance, the new pathways you may open in your life; like having a hill-top vantage point in the sea of options, swaying in the long soft grass. In a book shop though, there is a pressure to buy, and you can only find new pathways if you have a means to pay in that moment. A library though ... a library is both a sanctuary and a doorway to whole new worlds, and new and enriched versions of what we ourselves may be.

Whether you are reading this book in a book shop, a library, or relaxing somewhere, it may not be possible for you to reach out for another book or information right now, so I would like to take a moment here to have a few words with you about some words. I do not mean about the meanings or etymology of some words, but rather, their neurological impact and the dynamics they ignite within the recipient. When we talk to ourselves, we are the recipient of our own impactful language.

Some helpful words about words:

If there has been a moment in your life when someone you liked a lot said, 'I love you', for the very first time, a chain reaction would have been set in motion within your neurobiology: your heart rate changed, your blood pressure changed and to a certain degree your skin flushed with a little more red in response to your change in temperature. Your attitude to life changed, the fleeting pictures of your future that pass through your daydreams became rosier and 'smiley'. Your concept of 'where you were at' in life changed. A page turned and a new chapter began … remember?

It's a very different thing if someone you love says, 'I don't love you anymore'. A very different chemistry indeed.

While people use words all the time to convey ideas, few seem to be aware of the physiological, emotional or psychological effects their chosen words will have. By being in such a hurry just to get the communication done and 'out of the way', the intention of the original purpose is sometimes lost.

If, for example, our goal is to have another person empty a bin for us we already know that screaming abuse at them for fifteen minutes will get less of an enthusiastic response than simply asking politely, 'Could you empty the bin'?

Changing the wording slightly and adding the word 'please' on the end will yield a different feeling and inspire an even more cooperative response; 'Would you empty the bin please'?

For a more subtle example, to demonstrate the importance of the way we communicate:

'DON'T think of a big blue dog … with very bright yellow stripes'

Now, what did you just do?

Did you think of a big blue dog with very bright yellow stripes?

Of course you did, even though the request was for you to *not* do that.

The reason you thought of the dog was that, in order for your brain to process the meaning, your brain employs certain types of replicating cells, mirror neurons, to recreate within you that which your nervous system is feeding to your brain through the senses. To do this, your brain processes every word in every sentence and recreates, either consciously or non-consciously, the understanding it has of what is being conveyed.

Conscious minds can intellectualise negativity ; meaning they can contemplate the absence of something. To negate something means to remove it so that it becomes absent. Your unconscious processes positivity; meaning your unconscious only deals with what is 'there'; it can only process neural stimulus which exists. A mythos perspective might be to say that conscious minds have forward and reverse gears and your unconscious only has forward gears.

Do you remember in maths that a plus + and a minus - in an equation cancel each other out? $0 + 1 - 1 = 0$

In the sentence: 'DON'T think of a big blue dog with very bright yellow stripes' the plus and the minus in the word 'don't' cancel each other out.

Give this a go while you are reading this RIGHT NOW …

'Close your eyes without closing them'.

What happened?

Well, most of you having read that direct request will have not closed your eyes. This is because within that direct request there is an instruction to do something AND to not do something in the SAME sentence. Your unconscious deleted the information that was 'cancelling itself out' and only PROCESSED what was left afterwards.

'Close your eyes without closing them' = do something; *Not.*

So, if someone says to you, 'Don't be healthy' – your conscious mind can intellectually understand what is communicated ... and your unconscious will immediately begin to 'process' the ideas and concepts of 'being healthy', in order to identify what to not do.

Because you read the phrase, 'Don't be healthy', the negated-command is already happening and your unconscious now will explore any changes you need to become more healthy and look after yourself well, because your unconscious is adept at quickly identifying what you must do to ensure you treating yourself in the healthiest way possible has a great deal of importance for you, and your unconscious can figure out for itself when you can now make those changes and live a longer and healthy life. Now, the thing with 'process' is that human beings only tend to do something once they have processed an inclination.

Here's what I mean. Because right now you are reading these words you will continue to read these words, this book, forever, and ever, and ever ... and ever ... and ever until something specific happens: you will continue reading these words until you do something different, like take a break after reading this book and enjoy a blissful relaxing bath. Now, in order for you to do something else like enjoy a 'blissful relaxing bath' after reading this book, your brain has to send signals, at the appropriate time when you have finished reading, along your central nervous system to the muscles in your body to take on new shapes in readiness...then, as your muscles change shape and your body moves and animates itself towards having a blissful relaxing bath so too you will just find yourself enjoying the bliss of your relaxing bath after reading this book.

All action is preceded by a thought. It is impossible for you to do anything without thinking it first. Of course, some of your thoughts will be conscious and some of your thoughts will be unconscious. Now, saying something like, 'Don't be healthy' causes your unconscious to create scenarios, on the level of daydreams, or unconscious levels of fantasy, where the whole act of being healthy is mapped out – in detail – with all the timing and 'what to do' in place. Since your unconscious works so incredibly fast, the entire construct of 'being healthy' can be created in detail before your conscious mind has even noticed - all this happens inside your unconscious faster than you can consciously think of it. It is only a short step now to 'being healthy' being acted out physically.

So, saying 'Don't this', and 'Don't do that' to people can actually bring about the opposite result from the one you wanted. Because you thought you had communicated clearly, it often follows that when the 'opposite result' happens, there can be a (natural) tendency to assume that the opposite result that you got is a deliberate act of provocation by that person. Emotional and psychological defence mechanisms can then be activated and the defensive 'fight or flight' stress systems ignited.

Pheeeeew! ... all that explanation just for the sake of understanding the effect of one word, and yet it is very important to become aware of how to communicate effectively by fully understanding the impact of what and how you communicate – and the 'direction' you steer people in with every word and gesture you use.

I have seen a woman in a park whose young child is playing at the top of a climbing frame, look up and call out, 'Don't look down ... you'll fall ...' and guess what happened next.

I've known therapists do fantastic work with people and then, just as their client is leaving, say something like, 'Now don't you worry yourself ... '.

Some people ask: 'Well then, how can I get it right?' or, 'What if I wanted someone to not be late?'

Well, the answer is simple and yet somehow difficult for many people to achieve. In a modern society where people are used to stating things in negations, expressing oneself positively may take a bit of practice. Just ask them to do what you want them to do. Request, 'Please arrive on time'. It is easier to gain the co-operation of others if you ask them to do what you want them to do rather than go through a list of what you don't want them to do.

For another example, the word but. The word But tends to de-value whatever is said before it.

"You look great tonight, but …"

"I fully intend to re-pay you as soon as possible, but …"

Alternatively, the word 'And' connects sentences – and, therefore, it connects concepts and builds bridges between ideas and notions that seemed irreconcilable before.

"You look great tonight, and …"

"I fully intend to re-pay you as soon as possible, and …"

Courses in communication skills, like NLP and the more encompassing Neuro-Holistic Therapy , can be extremely useful in our social and private life as well as in the work place. Because mastering the art of rapport and communicating excellence is of such great benefit in every area of life.

Quite often people experience a 'split' between their conscious and unconscious agendas.

An obvious example might be that of a smoker who says they want to quit smoking, and yet continues to smoke. The conscious agenda is to stop. Their unconscious agenda (the behaviour driver) is to carry on, so even under their own protestations they continue to perform an 'unwanted' behaviour.

A less obvious example might be that of a person who has a conscious desire for close union and relationship while also having an unconscious desire for freedom and independence. This person might find themselves constantly drawn to people who can't, or won't, give commitment in relationships.

Having your conscious mind and your unconscious work in harmony together means your life will become easier and far more fulfilling. You will identify and achieve goals more easily and have that sense of 'feeling complete now' more often. It's time to open new pathways in your mind. This is often called in contemporary discourse, being authentic, or harmonious, or congruent.

First you begin to tune in to the truth of yourself. We all attach our own individual, subjective, meanings to words, concepts and ideas. It is as if, although we may speak English and the OED tells us the meanings of each word, we each have our own unique subjective, personal dictionary of meanings.

If you walk into an office and shout the word 'redundancy', you'll get one of two very different responses:

1. A slump in body posture coupled with the overall feeling the world has come to an end. The internal pictures are of all their hard won dreams shattering and melting into the despair of utter rejection and being useless.

2. Arms stretch up high to the ceiling with an overall feeling of elation. The internal voice shouts, "At last ! Now I am free to do what I've always wanted to do". The internal pictures are a thousand collages of steps to be taken, people to contact, points to remember … with an impatience to get on with it all as fast as possible.

So, is redundancy a bad thing? or, Is it a good thing?

Is redundancy a word that always has the same meaning for every person?

Or, is 'redundancy' just a word – our response to which we personally define as good or bad?

Some people believe themselves to be frightened of spiders.

Are they really?

People who are frightened of spiders very rarely go near them, let alone pick them up. In extreme cases these people will stay out of the kitchen all night to avoid a confrontation with one of these huge mean beasts. So, since they have no physical contact with them we can understand the sequence of the process to be like this:

Light from the surrounding environment bounces off the spider and into the observer's eye. Once there, it is transduced into an electrical signal which travels along various nerves to the brain. Next, it is transduced into an image. That image is then attributed with an identity and given a meaning. The observer then attributes an emotion with the meaning that has been given.

Questions present themselves:

Is the observer responding to the object, the spider on the outside?

or,

Is the observer responding to the meaning attributed to the image of the object?

If the observer is responding to the meaning, then is it possible to change the meaning?

Whose brain is in charge of the assignment of meanings given to words, ideas, thoughts, concepts and communications?

Indeed; it is yours, and since it is yours that is in charge it means that you can now, in your own time, go inside and adjust the meanings you associate with words, ideas, thoughts, concepts and communications to prompt the emotions and responses you want to experience and you consider to be far more productive for your life.

Like the response to the word redundancy, some people have a sense of excitement every time they return home to their loved ones. Some respond with enthusiasm and curiosity at the chance to learn and do something new. Some people find deliberately making the space to read and broaden their knowledge and understanding of this spiritual, emotional, psychological, physical, bio-chemical, scientific and creative experience of life is fun and easy to do.

There is a clear light, there is a way to open your mind to brighter new pathways …

I would like to ask you, is this kind of circular dialogue familiar?:

… 'Why?'

'Because I said so' …

'Why did you say so?' …

'Because I did!

Do remember that kind of thing?

As a kid it can be so frustrating to not get any straight answers. As an adult it can be so annoying to hear a constant 'Why?' 'Why?' 'Why?' …

Because different words create different responses and processes inside people, we're just going to take a moment to explore something that will help to make understanding yourself and others easier than it used to be. This will help in all your relationships.

The word 'Why' tends to cause people to become defensive.

When people hear that word 'Why' their unconscious immediately scans inside for reasons because the word 'why' seeks justification. It prompts the mind to identify the set of beliefs and associations that came together to create a situation/viewpoint. It challenges their point of view and brings out their weapons of verbal defence – an increasingly aggressive tone, faster rate of speech brought about through the faster breathing of the (now) activated 'fight or flight' mechanism.

Prompting a person to activate their fight and flight mechanism and become defensive and protectively aggressive as a result, is great if you just want loads of historical detail and no actual content, and it's fantastic if you want to cause a person to become more defensive because you are questioning the validity of their conclusions.

If you want actual content, if you want the person to reveal the model of their reality, a word which is different to 'why' is called for. Place the word 'What' at the beginning of the question and you will induce a different neural activity in the recipient and get a completely different response.

For example:

"Why did you do that?" – seeks justification and challenges their decision making.

"What was your reason for doing that?" – gives value, through implied acceptance, to their decision making abilities and asks to be let in on the secret of their success.

Now, it's time for you to notice just how important these things are in your life. You may have already begun to figure out for yourself how many uses communicating effectively will have for you. You might already have wondered how much better your relationships can be, how much more confident you will feel and how much easier it will be to move forward in life.

Very briefly:

The word ...

'What'   Initiates a search for   content

'How'   Initiates a search for   process

'When'   Initiates a search for   sequence

'Where'   Initiates a search for   context and   location

'Who'   Initiates a search for Identity or the performer

'Why'   Initiates a search for justification and defence

Whether a person verbally responds to these questions, or not, the process is always activated inside.

Along with you now using a voice that is encouraging and confident, how would it be useful for you to bring out a greater sense of co-operation from people?

Where will you use this knowledge ?

Who will benefit from you developing these skills and sharing what you learn ?

When are you going to explore your inner-mind learning these skills even further?

What action would you like to have taken around really developing your ability to communicate and influence with power and integrity, with compassion and clarity, and with a heightened intuition when you look back at your life three years from now in your future?

In a paper on language and conflict resolution I wrote:

Conflict transformation is an approach which recognizes conflict is a normal and continuous dynamic within human relationships' (Lederarch, 2003). The ability to take an alternative view, to re-position or re-frame the meaning of an event by adjusting the narrative with which we describe it, is an effective strategy for initiating relational change (Grinder & Bandler, 1981). Among many other possible models for resolving conflict Deutsch outlines an approach of non-violent communication. Initially, empathy rather than statements of evaluation are employed in a manner which maintains the status values of all parties concerned. The second stage is that of appreciative enquiry, using the style of questioning we have explored here, with a view to foster faith and cooperation alongside a mutual desire for change. Powerful non-defensive communication is advocated, suggesting communication be constructive and compassionate; relating is reciprocal and respectful (Deutsch et al, 2006).

There is so much more that can be presented for you than there is room for just here, and I would recommend as soon as your inner mind knows you have finished reading this healing works you will find yourself truly taking a positive step forwards to learn more about what you can achieve through mastering neuro-holistic approaches. There are new pathways waiting for you to step up to higher things. There is a great deal of information for you to consider developing your knowledge and transforming your life. That's one of the reasons why you are reading this book, and other books like it, is it not? With this in mind it is still important for you to remember this will open new pathways of change and success for you. Don't think about having to quickly accelerate your self-development right now. It's important you take all the time you need to make sure you now want to change and grow into being your own best self. When you know this is what you want, and you really know now is the time, you can take that step forward, can you not? When you do just imagine how good that will feel.

Everyone you meet has a perceptual filter: an inner bias to see, hear, and interpret the changing sensual world in a certain way. It is natural and OK to be different. Everything you experience is real in your subjective reality. Even the shared reality on the 'outside' changes as you change your viewpoint, and then changes your point of view. Since we all have a different angle on things it's easy if you become really curious, like an adventurous child, and discover another person's world - not through the old ways of making assumptions and guessing what people are thinking which always leads to more problems. Instead, now use these new ways of communicating to explore their inner world, encouraging them to feel valued. Use what you have learned already, and what you will learn in the future from your new pathways. When you take time to discover the inner world of another person you will find yourself being more valued than you can probably imagine. Taking time to wonder about yourself inside, and clarify issues through the art of communication, can ultimately save you a lot of time, energy, stress and grief ... literally ... think about it ...

In the world of positive thinking:

'Everything is positive'

When love = pain

a perspective on a Soul's nurtured aversion to loving intimacy

When a child's brain encounters the paradoxical pattern of incongruent care and forms an erroneous conclusion: love = pain

What do I mean by, 'incongruent care' ?

I'll first attempt a loose description, a kind of, 'working definition', firstly by describing 'congruent care'.

If congruence can be defined as, 'When words and actions match' (J. La Vale), then all parenting behaviours which are protective and also loving and also nurturing and also encouraging, guiding the young towards healthy independence and equipped to manage practically, intellectually, healthily, emotionally, spiritually, philosophically and economically, are congruent with the intention to parent well.

When our ancestors came down from the canopy and began to spread out across vast African plains, they were highly vulnerable. We hominoids have very small teeth and ineffective claws and we certainly can't outrun a large cat. The only chance we had for survival was the development of our frontal lobes; this huge lump of complex neuron-systems which gives us the ability to have a deep breadth of thought and to anticipate danger - we can think more steps ahead than a predator and outwit them. Pheeeeeeeeeeeew!

Sometimes, however, the young would frolic about and stray away from the group, moving far enough away that a swift moving predator can get in-between the young person and mum. We are the descendants of those who developed an intuitive emotional 'alarm' system, which some call, 'separation distress', and others call, 'attachment theory'. Whatever name you give it, this ingenious mechanism calls our feet to return to our 'secure base' as swiftly and expediently as possible.

Thousands of years later, we still have an innate piece of emotional elastic, pulling us towards whatever constitutes our 'secure base'. Bowlby called this, 'the Affectional Bond', and said, 'All affectional bonds are broken'. Meaning, that a mother cannot stay permanently physically attached

91

to her child. At some point, the connection with her will be broken; to answer the door, attend to cooking dinner etc. It is not the breaking of the affectional bond which leads to the formation of psychological and emotional problems later, but rather, the quality of their repair. Attachment therapists explore the roots of damaged or ruptured affectional bonds with a client, with the aim of helloing a person to reach the emotionally mature stage of internalising their secure base, so that the sense well being is then with them as they walk the up and down path of life with its challenges and joys.

There is a current body of thought emerging from the revision of Psychotherapy from the findings in Interpersonal Neurobiology and Affective Neuroscience, that all psychopathologies have their roots in Affect Dysregulation, brought about by corrupted or poorly repaired affectional bonds. The observed dynamics are often referred to as, 'Attachment Schemes'.

There is another dimension to the challenges of our innate sense of security and healthy sense of self esteem; what if, just what if, the adult we are attached to and seek loving care from is problematic in themselves ?

What happens to our relationship with love, with kindness, with caring and loving ourselves, if a parent is absent, careless, clumsy, unkind or even emotionally or psychologically cruel or violently abusive?

I am not going to recount them here, but in my work I hear harrowing accounts of neglect and mistreatment and one wonders why some parents bother to become parents at all. But then, one remembers biology, which reminds me to remember to tell you something ...

In social media, such as Facebook, we often see pre-made postcard type pictures which have some kind of inspiration quote or philosophical advice, passing through our news feeds. Some people call these, 'memes', however, the term meme has another, deeper connotation.

You may have heard of Richard Dawkins the atheist; his day job is being a Professor of Biology at Oxford University. In his 1989 book, 'The Selfish Gene', he proposed a theory of a secondary lineage of inheritance; not one of biology, but of culture, concepts, beliefs, philosophy, narrative and discourse. He called these, 'Memes'. Think of them as a kind of psychological-gene, which can be passed down from generation to generation. Families which live in the same street and speak the same native language, each use that language differently, whether speaking Spanish, Welsh or English, the individual family usage of that language will differ, very slightly, from that of their neighbours. Small niche groups have learned phrases, figures of speech, in-jokes that outsiders 'won't get'.

Psychological dispositions are also observed, copied, learned and then passed down by oneself to one's own children.

On a personal note, I am rather fond of a song lyric written by Thomas Dolby:

'So check beneath your fingernails,

In between your toes,

Right between your earlobes darling,

That's where culture grows ... '

The culture of the landscape of our psyche pre-determines not just what we do, but how we see, hear and comprehend the world around us. We introject our emotional and psychological family environment, compute the 'making of meaning' through its lenses, and then intraject our reactions and responses out into the world around us.

What happens if, when we feel the elastic within us pulling our feet to run towards our parent, our guide, our protector, that the person we are running to is also dangerous to our well being?

It would be like being propelled towards a giant soft lovely-smelling ball that has poisoned spikes sticking out of it.

A child on the receiving end of incongruent care is caught within a paradox, 'love + pain', which often results in confusion, guilt, rage and a bedlam of mixed emotions which often result in self-sabotaging behaviours; frustration, self loathing and self love in a jumble.

A parent is not just a person we love, they are also our teacher, our guide, and our life-support system. We are biologically wired to go towards our parents in open receptivity, seeking the rewards of loving care, food, water shelter and protection.

Can you imagine the resulting confusion and bewilderment, if the support system is painful? ... the narrative criticising instead of encouraging ? ... the behaviour violent instead of comforting ? ... the proximity dangerous and life-threatening instead of nurturing and protective?

The child may feel it wants to run away from the pain and yet it will die if not in close proximity to the supportive adult. The child then may come to hate that which is expected to be loving but demonstrates the opposite, and come to learn to hate a person it loves whilst always being biologically wired to love the same person it hates.

Like all human emotions, this has a dynamical rage; a wide spectrum of possibilities.

A parent may not realise that their level of sensitivity is difference to their child's and consider themselves to be they are 'just playing', 'just joking', 'just as we have always done in our family', and not realise the effect it has in the secret inner realm of the child's unconscious emotions. The very idea that they are uncaring or unsupportive might be abhorrent to them, and yet, if they were to play very close attention to their child's experience, they may find that how they are perceived is different to their own notion of themselves.

At the other end of the scale, there are sometimes parents who consciously and wilfully participate in acts of bullying or abuse of their own children.

This is a wide spectrum; from parents who sexually abuse a child, to those who are playfully sarcastic, mums who talk on the phone instead of initially making eye contact with a heart-smile into their child's eyes, to parents who are frustrated and resort to various types of punishment in an attempt to cajole a child into 'learning' and 'behaving themselves' (which I think means, 'the child no longer inconveniently disturbs what I am doing').

For some children, the absence of a parent can carry the sting of deep rejection alongside the confusion. The death of a parent can also bring about the formation of the following equation in the unconscious mind:

love = pain

A child whose unconscious forms the equation love = pain may have a variety of problems when forming relationships in their future.

If love means pain, then the person's clever brain may form strategies, below the conscious level of awareness, to avoid love at all costs. Fire = pain; avoid fire. Falling from a height = pain; avoid falling. Love – pain; avoid love.

This can be done in a variety of ways;

In close intimate relationships:

A sour disposition – 'vinegar don't bring the bee'.

Forming relationships with people who are perhaps 'good enough', but do not melt one's heart with love.

Forming relationships for financial or practical, security reasons to, 'escape' from one's circumstances.

An incongruent and inconsistent manner of relating; black and white, chalk and cheese, Jekyll and Hyde. This creates a push-me-pull-you dynamic, a kind of, 'come away closer ... '

Forming relationships with people who are 'just about good enough', but also have glaring flaws and faults, so the dynamic is 'come here and let me criticise you and then be angry with you if you change while also being disappointed with you if you do not change'

Remember; the objective of one part of the psyche is to avoid love, because it is dangerous to open one's heart and trust. Whilst at the same time, another part of the psyche yearns for close union and relationship; we are relational creatures after all.

Rather than diving into the pool of deep intimacy, working through old learned habits of pain and releasing the repressed emotions from the system, a person can, for years, or even a whole life time, continue to hold the pains within their unconscious and have only a half-hearted depth of intimacy with others as a result. This also means only a partial intimacy with knowing oneself ...

and, in relationship with oneself:

A propensity to make life endangering decisions.

A desire for constant external distractions, to avoid 'feeling' one's self.

A paradox of disliking the self and yet also feeling angry when others de-value or express dislike for ourself.

There are many more permutations and, while this list is not comprehensive by any means, the environment of this book holds little space for such a depth of enquiry or study, it does, I hope, serve as a guide and give you a flavour for the dynamics of something a lot of people experience.

Can 'love = pain' be changed ?

Yes!!

Neuroscience also shows that the brain is plastic; meaning that it is changeable in nature. If our brain learns the painful equation at one point in our lives, then we can teach it a new paradigm at a different time in our lives.

In my therapeutic work, Neuro-Holistic Therapy, a synthesis of NLP and Hypnotherapy and Psychobiology (Mind-Body Healing), language, both verbal and non-verbal, is used to help your unconscious identify the root causes of issues and bring about enduring and lasting change. Wounds are healed, conundrums resolved, paradigms shifted and doors to New Pathways are open ... :)

Love = joy; kindness, growth, success, delight, self-care, other-care, respect, and to honour one's unique part in creation.

When would Now be a good time for you to give yourself permission to learn to begin feeling wonderful?

A trio of painful emotions

... we have evolved to help the Soul to learn and grow deeper in wisdom, compassion and love; 3 intensely powerful 'Soul learning' tools

There is a theoretical school of Psychology which views human behaviours from a perspective of natural selection. Human behavioural traits such as altruism, selfishness, jealousy, sarcasm, shyness, etc are not seen as good or bad things in their own right, but rather, as adaptive behaviours, responses and reactions which perform some kind of function. This perspective is known as Evolutionary Psychology.

Evolutionary Psychology suggests that just as biological patterns and functions endure in a species until it becomes necessary for them to adapt to changes or mutate, psychological patterns of behaviours, traits and psychopathologies only continue in humans because they perform some kind of function which is both efficient and significant to the organism's ongoing process of maintaining equilibrium and surviving. According to this viewpoint, if a trait or response does not have efficacy for the system as a whole, then it would pass from the human experience and be consigned to history.

There are some emotional responses that occur in our relationships which are often given valance, or a sense of value which carries an emotional weight, and are often experienced as; bad, horrible, negative, unwanted, sickening, disgusting, awful, terrible just plain wrong.

I am not going to suggest that we perform a Shakespearian revolution and make a glorious summer from such wintery discontents, but it can be useful to have an alternative perspective which fosters insight into our relationship with life which may also reduce the intensity of an emotional sting.

The words, the emotions, we are about to discuss may carry a powerful affective charge. They may carry a variety of feelings and memories which may be unpleasant to consider or hold. If you find yourself feeling discomfort I would recommend you stop reading for a little while and immediately turn your attention to doing something simple that you enjoy; put the kettle on, go for a short walk, play some favourite music or speak with a dear close friend who makes you laugh.

Guilt:

When was I 15 years old, early in 1978, I started following an amazing, innovative and intelligent band called Siouxsie and the Banshees. They didn't have a recording contract at the time and you could only hear their music through John Peel on the BBC or by seeing them live. For months I saw them as often as I could in dingy dives, violent town halls and even an ex mortuary; a fitting venue for the spirit of goth to come.

Their first album was like a major cultural event for those of us in the original punk scene, now being swept along in the new wave of a 'post punk' identity crisis. New bands were emerging all the time: Magazine, The Fall, Joy Division, Monochrome Set; I jammed with the Monochrome Set once in a guitar shop in Denmark Street one Saturday afternoon, about 2 weeks after a spent a day at Here and Now's house in Iver Heath. These new bands were changing the tone of the cultural landscape and the Banshees second album, Join Hands, seemed dark and brooding. The Car Crash rhythms of The Scream had given way to a more Metal Postcard, as if the band themselves were expressing a Suburban Relapse in musical form.

Among the tracks on Join Hands was a rather exuberant song called Icons. It was a polemic against Catholic conditioning: 'Icons feed the fires, Icons falling from the spires', but there was something else...

Enmeshed into the exquisite jangling guitars was a sweet refrain: 'the guilt is golden, the gilt is golden'...

I loved this song with a passion and it is still in my top 100 songs of all time.

Jump forwards many years to Ramsbury in east Wiltshire, England, and I am in a Neuro-Holistic Therapy session with a new client who is caught in a tangle of guilt and self recrimination. I suddenly remembered the Banshees' song and thought, 'I wonder what is of Value here?'

What possible purpose can guilt perform?

How is guilt useful?

How is guilt your friend?

How does guilt enable you to survive more easily and how does it help us thrive?

What is the *function* of guilt?

If we place to one side our cultural understanding of guilt and suspend our personal history of incidents of felling guilty, what one may find is that guilt is a word which we use to describe a particular sensation we experience in our body; often located in the heart area or in our tummy.

The sensation we call guilt tends to be evident when we are engaged in a certain activity. Often, it is the activity of taking a path which leads us away from a previously desired destination. The sensation we call guilt also arises if we embark on a course of action which is disruptive, harmful, disturbing or even destructive towards something which, in our hearts, we hold in high value. An esotericist would describe the sensation as a signal from our soul, or wise inner being, that is calling our attention to be mindful of a potential error of judgement.

It is as if our inner self is attempting, like a dog tugging at our heels, to catch our conscious mind's attention, saying, 'hey, conscious mind, this action takes you on a different path to that which you have previously set within your heart ... are you sure this what you want to do'??

We can only feel guilty about something that matters to us - if it isn't important to us we will not experience the heavy sensation we call guilt.

In whichever way you wish to think of it, we only guilt that which is golden.

I would highly recommend that you listen to the messages in your body which emanate from the heart of your feelings and perhaps re-assess your decisions so that your feet walk your path upon light wings.

Shame:

This discussion is on the word, 'Shame'. It is not a discussion on being 'ashamed', or, nor of being made to 'be ashamed' from an external source for being naturally human. Some interpretations of certain religious texts, for example, have given ruthless people permission to manipulate and control the behaviours of other people, often to their detriment. The act of invoking this powerful emotion for one's own ends, to the detriment of another, is, in its mildest form, bullying and repugnant to my compassionate nature.

Given the powerful cultural associations which come laden with this word, how can we approach investigating the neurological usefulness of shame, as far as your brain is concerned.

What is the *function* of shame?

Shame is the name we give in English to identify a specific affective or emotional experience; the voluntary dampening down of inner joy. What we call shame is a primary mechanism within our voluntary social civilizing behaviours; such as apologising for a mistake, correcting typos, paying for goods instead of stealing them, asking for consent instead of raping and not spitting in public just whenever we feel like it.

In the first two years of life we experience exuberant affect surging through our system, manifesting mostly as the emotion of joy. When feel this when mum touches us, holds us, when we hear her voice, look into her eyes and smell her smell.

We ingest things; food and drink - Joy!

We discard things - metabolised waste from food and drink - Joy!

We are encouraged to just 'be'.

Until ...

A time comes when our joy at exuberantly discarding waste is not met with joy but with disdain. The look on mum's face, the tone in her eye, the shrill in her voice resonates with a disappointment that could potentially migrate into a death-bringing abandonment; this is very scary.

Allan Schore reports in *Affect Dysregulation and Disorders of the Self*, that the misatunement of joy being met with disgust, or connection being met with a painful distress state which includes an inhibition of dopamine in the brain and cardiac deceleration . The distress is painful to endure and the desire to reconnect in joyful attunement is so strong that we turn our attention to seeking reconnection by adapting our behaviour as quickly as possible to regain the state of equilibrium and the sensation of being loved.

Often, our first experience of adjusting our natural biology in order to fit with the requirements of an external observer, first mum, then family, then society, is called 'potty training'. From a parental-Dawinian perspective, the act of 'shaming', or, of intense disapproval in real-time, is useful in a Pavlovian-training way for a parent to stop a child running into the road or putting its hand into a flame. If it is repeated with kindness and the reconnection and attunement restored in a joyful loving way, then the distress signal is quickly transduced into a signal for action and the new learned behaviour of voluntary self adjustment.

In this very moment, we step from being a creature of biology into a person of cizilised social attunement. We are relational beings and being able to regulate our own affect is an important part of how we relate with ourselves and the world.

Experiencing this function of neurobiology can be uncomfortable at times, but then no one ever said that being a Soul in Earth school is easy. The feeling of inwardly learning is often accompanied with a rise in the feeling of temperature, as if the adjustment in affect turns up our inner heat. We may feel, 'hot under the collar', when we take the exam, go for the interview and place a lot of important hopes on, 'getting it right'. The little awkward feeling I have when I spot the typo after a social media posting, the hot temperature I feel when I forget the next line of a song while I am singing to an audience, are the sensations of my inner self learning in real-time so that on future occasions I am more mindful and more full of care

I mentioned at the start of this discussion that if an adult uses a person's propensity to feel shame, or a culture employs shame, to force or coerce adults and children to do their bidding in ways which serve the needs of the shamer and not the needs of the learner, then this is tyrannical and impositional and deserves to be considered shameful, in my opinion. I wish bullies and tyrants and impositional cultures which employ both guilt and shame as psychological and emotional weapons with which to nudge, push and cajole people into fitting with their narrow lens of how people 'should' be were able to be ashamed of such bullying behaviour. My reason for saying this is that in order for a bully to learn that imposition is unkind and unwise, they need to experience the sensation of, 'I am doing something wrong', in real time, at the time they are doing it, which carries such an affective or emotional charge that it causes them to immediately stop and change their behaviour. This would be known as a bully learning to be kind, a savage learning to be wise, an institution learning to hold those in its sphere.

I have more of a liking for carrots than sticks, and I can understand the mechanism of shouting 'Stop!!', as a child is running towards the edge of the pavement is like a shock to the system for the child in that moment, and yet it is delivered with passionate love and a desire to protect and care. Sometimes, early, infant, boundary-rules are very useful in childhood but can also become a hindrance if they are not discarded through adolescence; voluntary self regulation is a completely different thing to being vulnerable and fearfully responding to an impositional bully.

From an evolutionary perspective, our neurobiology is concerned with affective arousal and seeking homeostatic equilibrium for the system has a whole. This functional process isn't concerned with the valance of emotion, nor of the context. However, within milliseconds the affective charge is registered in consciousness and transducers into emotion. Now it has quality, valance and a sense of feeling good... or not.

If I spot the typo myself, and self edit, before I post on live social media, I feel good.

If I am mocked by someone else for making the typo, after posting on social media, I feel embarrassed and awkward for overlooking the error, or being in a hurry, or being dyslexic, or, in fact, for not conducting myself at the perfection level of my self-expectation.

I do not feel shame though; I feel a different emotion.

Regret:

Regret can be experienced as a heavy sensation in the heart and sometimes in the tummy. Sometimes it is experienced as heat, but most often has a 'dread cold' about it. Regret has a relationship with both shame and guilt. Think of these three as inner-guide teachers of Time.

Guilt; a sensation we experience when we are about to stray away from a path which is of value to our heart or soul - Before we do the behaviour.

Shame; a sensation we experience when we are about to stray away from a path which is of value to our heart or soul - Before we do the behaviour.

Regret; a sensation we experience when we are about to stray away from a path which is of value to our heart or soul - Before we do the behaviour.

One antidote to regret is creative, imaginative planning. When we realise that we have behaved in a way that is different from our deepest values or highest ideal, what steps can we now take to change direction and return to the path which feels congruent and good inside?

Sometimes, we may find ourselves unable to change or undo the behaviour we are regretting and either look for a new pathways which will somehow make amends or take us to a feeling of redemption. We may have to follow the advice of CG Jung:

'Sometimes a problem cannot be solved; it can only be outgrown.'

Soul Mates - Disappointment - The Golden Palace Under the Sea

Some people believe there is a soul-mate for every person. During my therapeutic career I have met many people who are forlorn at having lost their soul-mate, or in despair at not having yet found 'the one'. I have met some who believe they have found their soul mate and others who believe there is more than one... or none.

If we think of the philosophy of Souls incarnation and learning through interactions with other Souls; whether that is daily or occasionally, there is a high chance that some Souls will meet with a sense of pre-life arrangement. The nature of quality of that arrangement is variable, ranging from magic and amazing to dreadfully terrible, the worst of human experience.

Generally, the term Soul-mate describes an intimate relationship which has a strong bond or feel which each person can only describe as 'spiritual', as if some divine hand were at play upon their meeting. 'We clicked immediately', I knew from the very start', are wonderful for those fortunate enough to have such experiences.

I have met people who seem to spend life haunted by the quest to find a love never found, as if they are cast adrift on planet Earth and their Soul love is not here.

My recommendation would be to change one's approach and inner narrative. Rather than look for 'the one', be aware instead of the degree or depth of 'oneness' which is constituted by every relationship we form.

Soul-mate type connections can seem incredibly powerful and we can be swept away by love. This is wonderful, incredible and amazing and also imbued with idealism. It may be wise to be aware that it is possible to project one's desire for an ideal onto another person and instead of relating with them as if they are a person, relate with them instead as if they are a Goddess or a God. We may strike lucky and find such a God or Goddess - fantastic.

Then again, we might not; our beautiful deity can fall off the pedestal and come crashing down into disappointment and we can fall into a heart-crushing disappointment. Idealism in general is a wonderful thing, though it can set up expectations which exceed perfectionism.

Imagine for a moment that you could see all things clearly for what they are, as if you have a clear memory of the place your Soul resided in before you came into life and the place to which you will return when life here is done. You could well find yourself looking out onto a world with angels running around with machine guns.

For many who have moments of spiritual insight, the gap between 'what is', and, 'what could be', can be crushing.

We may seek to offset this disappointing divine homesickness by feeling driven to make the world 'out there' as wonderful as the world we know it could be. Acts of kindness and compassion can be the by product of a Soul wanting to literally make Earth like Heaven.

The inspired arts can be a place to turn to; forms of spiritual healing, hypnotherapy, meditation, or losing oneself in art, dance, photography or drama. We may literally dispel the blues by playing them. Alternatively, we can mask the clarity and let a fog cloud it over, becoming lost inside fantasy or movies or television, or even experience a kind of Soulful shell-shock and just seem to drift off somewhere ...

Other seek chemical escape routes to numb the pain of life; I am sure you do not need me to list chemicals which change our emotions and state of consciousness.

There is a legend in Greek in mythology which may offer a sense of purpose if you are experiencing any degree of divine homesickness.

It was said that when Neptune, the god of the oceans and all waters, emerged from the sea he would do so in three classic ways;

At times the seas around him would be calm and clear.

Sometimes he would be accompanied by wild tempests and furious storms, not unlike how we are sometimes swept away by our passions.

At other times, he would be accompanied by fog, and Sirens would call sailors upon the winds and their boats would be dashed to pieces on the rocks.

It was said that Neptune had a golden palace under the sea and anyone who enters this place instantly feels a complete spiritual attunement akin to what some call nirvana, for atonement, or ascension. It is a state in which we feel completely connected with the entire universe, experiencing no loneliness, hurt or any pain.

If this sounds wonderful to you, I agree!

The only problem is, that to get to Neptune's golden palace you have to drown. You do not drown in water, but rather, in disappointment.

If we are able to refrain from making it and creating a verity of anaesthetic distractions, the pain we feel softens the heart. This bruising is not like being hurt by a person deliberately, it is as if nature or life itself, as if the fates have done it. Allowing oneself to feel if softens the heart and we become more compassionate, more spiritually sensitive and attuned as a result.

You may remember the metaphor or the stadium-dartboard; if we find ourselves feeling a deep sense of disappointment with someone; perhaps we have been let down or life went down an unforeseen path...

Sometimes we expect people to behave in certain ways, not because we have observed them and made well-informed conclusions, but rather because we want them to fit in with an idea of what we want them to be, instead of relating with them for who they actually are. Relating with a desired idea of a person, and not with the actual person, is a pathway to disappointment and its consequential unhappiness and pain. If you want a person to be a certain way with you, and they are being different to how you wish, stop and ask yourself what is it about this person, among all the 7 billion currently on Earth, that means you have to hurt yourself with self-inflicted disappointment?

What would happen if you identified the qualities you need and then looked for them in other people who are already in that place to share them with you?

What changes do you need to make within you in order for such sharing to become more likely?

However you personally define your level of self esteem, it can be helpful to decide for yourself that you are intrinsically special and deserve only the best in life; this includes the best nutrition for your heart. Decide to stop accepting anything that is detrimental or even toxic in your life. Decide you are now only going to enjoy the very best heart food.

If you are walking to the top class restaurant of life one can feel hungry while taking such a walk; the path may even pass some fast food outlets and it can be very tempting to step in and satisfy one's immediate hunger. However, once such an immediate hunger has been reduced, the drive to continue walking to the best restaurant can fade and we can become entrenched in an unsatisfactory, or even heart-poisonous, relationship.

Given the choice between a quick-fix and the continued walk along the path of loneliness to that which is loving nutrition for your heart is tough, I know, I absolutely understand how an 'it'll do for now', relationship can alleviate the immediate pain of loneliness but, ultimately, being in a relationship with someone who doesn't make your heart burst into a smile and your Soul glow, just by them even being near you, can mean one feels lonely while already in a relationship; and that can be painful and even self harming (emotionally).

It takes courage to risk loneliness in favour of only accepting what is best for you. It takes courage to open your heart and embrace love when its light illumes your world. A deep breath then, and a decision to love your life as it is, or, change your life into becoming a life you love.

We have found happiness is more of an orientation, a heart-direction, than an event. Set your heart to love by first loving you.

Will love find me though?

What if it is not meant to be?

What if I am meant to be stuck with this person?

What if it is not my destiny to find true real love?

Such questions demand our attention, do they not?

Fate and Free-will

Destiny and the Power to Change

You may already know, I have been a student of Astrology since 1982, and a practitioner and teacher of Astrology since 1991. Astrologers are often asked about concepts like fate, destiny and things which are 'meant to be' …

'What is my path in life'? … 'What am I 'meant' to do'?

This is so prevalent in the discourse surrounding Astrology that it is one of the key themes I address in my online Introduction course; The Dynamics of Astrology:

Is everything fated?

If the answer is 'yes', this suggests we are nothing but puppets, living out the scripted imaginings of some external deity (who seems to have been watching far too many soap operas on television). If this is the case, it would mean astrology is pointless. If our lives are scripted, and we are pulled around by some puppeteer of consciousness then looking at charts for insight and foresight becomes irrelevant: if we can't change anything, why bother looking?

or…

Do we have free will?

Do we have an existential free will in which all possibilities are open to us, regardless of their degree of probability?

If the answer is 'yes', astrology is then rendered useless because it becomes a something limiting, like a straight jacket around one's potentials.

However, this dualistic perception of; 'free will, or, fate', is also somewhat illusory. The human condition is far more sophisticated and complex than something so black or white.

In 2008 I posted a Facebook note outlining my understanding of fate and free-will, or at least, my understanding at the time of writing. In 2009 I had to choose a topic for my masters degree in Psycho-Social Studies and I wanted to take the opportunity to investigate something very specific.

During the Msc we were taught a module on Affective Neuroscience and Systems Theory which opened up a whole new world of understanding for me. Writing about brain anatomy at masters degree level meant my own sense of identity had to change and my self esteem grew as a result. For the dissertation in 2009 I decided to address something that I had read in an Astrology many years before. In *The Moment of Astrology*, a fantastic book by the way, Geoffrey Cornelius ridicules a ley tenet of natal, or birth chart, Astrology; the a person's trajectory of character is determined or set in motion by the environment (celestial sphere) which surrounds a person at the time of their first breath.

This discrediting of a 'seed moment', caused some astrological readers to abandon the whole notion of a birth chart altogether and fundamentally altered their mode of practice. However, this was not the case with myself, or any of my students. In 1991, at the start of my practice and teaching career, I have been employing a model of Astrology that I created in January 1991. It is called Astrobiography and, in a nutshell, views a person's life as a series of distinct chapters, each of which has its own dynamics, tone, atmosphere and general sense of experience. Each chapter of life rests upon the one before it and colours, or informs, the one that follows. It is possible to use Astrology as a language of polysemus symbols which describe the overarching archetypical journey of a person's life path in addition to describing the structure of their subjective experience in every area of life. Astrological symbols are rich in layers of meaning and in client work I help a person to explore not just how a certain area of life is currently happening for them, but we also other plausible possibilities for approaching that area of life. In the way that I and other professional astrologers use it, Astrology is an invaluable tool for insight. This of course suggests that a birth chart is not static, and also that the meanings one can draw from a birth chart are not static and 'carved in stone' either. If even Astrology is not a tool of fate, is anything in human experience 'fated'?

To address this question, we can look at fate and free-will through 2 different 'lenses'; Mythos and Logos.

Logos - logic; a left-brain perspective.

Mythos - imaginal narrative; a right-brain perspective.

For Logos, if you would like to see the details of the MSc investigation, Determinism and Agency is Affective Neuroscience, please see the book; *How We Come into Being* by me, David Charles Rowan.

For our journey here though, Mythos:

Imagine a field of soft tall grass, gently swaying in a light summer breeze:

A rabbit makes its way through the grass, hopping around any deep pools of water or even quicksand. No sooner has the rabbit made its way through the grass, the wind gently blurs the pathway once more; grass tops swaying in the rhythm of the wind ...

If, however, a second rabbit follows the same path as the first, before the wind has diffused the trail, the pathways navigating the swamp would become a little more firmly established and may begin to retain their visibility, even in a stronger wind.

If a human comes along and also desires safe passage across this unknown terrain, a choice is presented;

a) Walk blindly across the grassland in any direction of one's choosing, knowing that with each step one's life may be at risk

or ....

b) Cautiously follow the rabbit trail, knowing that it shows safe passage.

If this path is then walked many times by lots of human feet, the path may become so well established that someone may decide to lay gravel and stones and broaden the path, enabling a horse and cart to make safe journey. Eventually someone invents tarmac and cars, and the road is firmly set. Or at least, set until it is changed.

The neuroscientist Daniel Dennet spoke of selectionism in consciousness. In a Darwinian sense, neural networks are established from de-selecting from thousands of possibilities, which then fade away to leave behind the trail already followed. Edelman and Tonini speak of reentry, in the book, *Consciousness; How Matter Becomes Imagination*, describing how repetitions of neural activity reinforce choices or responses already made.

In short; our past carves out neural pathways which we experience as narrative; the narrative is the manner in which we describe and comprehend our reality which we then emotionally and behaviourally respond to as if it is true. However, it is possible to open new pathways of thoughts and responses at any time. Changing the narrative and opening new pathways is not easy and takes certain skill; spiritual disciplines which practice repeated meditation and chanting, neuro-linguistic technologies like CBT, Hypnotherapy, NLP and Neuro-Holistic Therapy work at the coal face of reframing our interpretation of circumstances so new pathways are now available ...

If, 'all the world's a stage and we are but merely players', then we are also the producer, the director,, the script writer and we are even in charge of casting (yes, we are … this crew you share your life with; you are the Simon Cowell of their auditions).

We may have an awareness or our potential flexibility in choosing our destination, or destiny; or not. How we meet life plays a role in the quality of experience, the quality of life we build for ourselves.

To borrow from weather for a moment:

If we know an individual has planned to have a picnic next Sunday and in their part of the world, the forecast is that Sunday will be a windy day, the person has a range of choices in how to respond to the forecast news.

Depending on a person's temperament, values, beliefs, emotional needs, habits and desires, some people might dig their heels in, attempt to defy the wind and chase paper plates around a field all afternoon. Another, somewhat more flexible and perhaps wiser soul, may change their plans/pathway/destination/destiny and decide to take advantage of the wind; go to the kite festival and have a fantastic Sunday afternoon!

In my current understanding, fate and free-will co-exist and are different functions of temporal comprehension. Liz Greene said in a lecture that fate is to do with the past and destiny the future.

The past does not exist anymore, it is as if dust on the wind. The future is truly just a set of possibilities. However, our relationship with the past may colour and distort the clarity with which we are able to perceive and interpret the meaning of the present. The future, while not carved in stone, is in line with a certain trajectory and it is possible, with good skill, to perceive the orientation of one's path and gain a sense of where it is heading.

Enjoy the path you are on or learn how to change it if you need to. You already know how to make life be a certain way: you are living out the choices you have already made in your history right now. However, you are not necessarily stuck with your lot. It is the nature of life for things to change, sometimes slowly and sometimes quickly, but change is guaranteed and new pathways are available for you. Whether your guide is your own instinctive intuition, a deity of a religion or a wise person with a capacity for both insight and foresight, it is possible to learn how to re-direct your feet to take new pathways.

We are helped by nature; the human brain is capable of creating new brain cells - yes, brand new thoughts you have never though before. The process is called, Neurogenesis. The brain itself is plastic, meaning that it changes and is able to change its architecture; which means new thoughts, which means new realities. It is amazing ...

We are amazing...!

You are amazing...!!

Contemplation ...

... and the thin cord of Astral Light joined the Soul to the fertilised egg that lay within the Gateway, spinning like a galaxy.

... and so he ventured into this new living journey, replenished and equipped with talents and flaws, gifts and vulnerabilities, with an ideal agenda of what to accomplish set deep inside his inner-mind. Long dimmed were the voices of the Great Wise, and yet his feelings still were haunted by the echoes of their knowing.

At different times during his living lessons, his life, his inner mind heard and recognised the truths of the Great Wise as if being awoken by some 'other-worldly tuning-fork'. His inner being resonated to the truths that shone as sunlight through every tunnel of trees, carried upon the laughter of children like waves of a gentle hand whispering, 'remember ...'. Sometimes, he caught glimpses of it staring back at him in a mirror, and often he felt it when he opened his heart to another in romantic love.

In lonely times, and hours of confusion he sought for it. He thought he found it once in a book considered by many many people to be the correct ways of truth, yet for him, there was something, well, missing in their words and actions that he felt should have been there .... although he had no idea what that 'something' should be. At one time he desperately searched in the bottom of many wine glasses, and no matter for how long he stared he could not find it in a television. He looked for it in the art that so many said portrayed it, and in the tapestry of sounds and rhythms that radiated from the vibrant talent all around him. He found it neither in the town or countryside or in any land he searched, for a part of him always felt somehow detached from the world, separate from the people in it, kind of 'to-one-side' of people.

And so, as he journeyed, like a droplet of spirit flowing out towards some vast ocean of eternity, there came the time when the echoes resonant within his inner mind would begin to whisper more often in his dreams; almost as if an immortal inner-light within his very being was gently waking him as time was drawing nearer the time when waking would once again be but a dream, softly calling him, 'Home'.

We do not need to wait until journey's end to touch the inner light, and nor do we need to drown in disappointment in order to step inside Neptune's golden palace beneath the sea.

We can, just for a few moments, a few moment each day if you wish, lift the eye of our attention away from the physical, dizzying external world of noise and movements and visions and the feelings within us which rise and fall upon the undulating wave of our moods and satisfactions.

You can place the eye of your attention on that which is utterly beautiful ... for you.

rest this book with this page open, where you can still see it ... and read this text slowly, deliberately, mindfully ...

and gently breathe, in ... and out ... and continue to breathe and read slowly ...

and settle into feeling comfortable because, in a moment, you are going to experience a level of relaxation will, create the environment, inside, where your unconscious can begin, to experience a wonder... full ... spiritual energy just flows through you all the time, and now it's time, for you begin to learn, really learn, just how, so easy it can be to relax ...

and to know, and to experience ...

relaxing just enough to begin to remember how much,

you enjoy the pleasure of relaxing with your eyes open in a deep daydreaming way ...

your breathing becoming easier,

and deeper, your unconscious, drifting now, into relaxation,

some call meditation, some call spiritual, some call profoundly mystical - now, hear,

you can relax even deeper,

so just think of your left foot ... and your right foot ...

and as you drift deeper now think of your right hand ... and your left hand ...

and there's a part of you that remembers the stars,

and that part of you can take you now into a light ... floating kind of feeling,

and while you relax deeper now, your unconscious remembering the stars,

like remembering looking at all the stars in a beautiful night sky,

and it's just you,

drifting into more and more comfort as you remember looking at the stars and finding one star,

just singling out one star that's a little bit larger,

a little bit brighter than all the rest,

like you were picking out a private star,

a private world,

and you relaxing even deeper now as that light,

floating, drifting towards that light from that star just floating gently, ... peacefully, quickly closer and closer, and deeper, and warmer,

as the light from that star begins to shine more and more,

as you flow into profound, comfort, sensations of finding that as you drift in the light, of this star,

you only find that which is beautiful for you, the light of that star is only filled with whatever is beautiful for you, and you can enjoy now, this time in that star,

just enjoy relaxing, your mind flowing with whatever is beautiful for you ....'

and enjoy now; the thoughts, the feelings, the visions the memories of only that which is beautiful for you ...

and now, as your unconscious remembers,

and those feelings you enjoyed become more pleasing, stronger now as you begin to gently drift, and return, just drifting down, and down, and down,

drifting down like a little feather sinking down through, warm air, until, you find, you are feeling,

all those enjoyable feelings, and thoughts, and visions that were beautiful,

in your body once more, as, in your own time now,

you remember your left hand ... and your right hand ... and your right foot ... and your left foot ...

filled with the essence of all that is beautiful for you,

for your soul, that inner you as you return to normal consciousness conscious of the beauty,

and the star -t .

For you I'd paint the stars

I looked out far into the night

And darkness met my eye ...

I plunged a ladder into the earth

and climbed up to the sky

up and up, up through the clouds

past the Moon and then past Mars ...

upon the velvet sky for you

I did paint a billion stars ...

Beauty ... full

There are no wrinkles in your soul ...

There are no wrinkles in your heart ...

There are no wrinkles in your eyes ...

There are no wrinkles in your beautiful sacred space ...

There may be bruises, scratches, bumps and batterings from time spent in this temporal realm and your eyes may be clouded with pain, your heart may be deeply bruised, your soul may carry a weight which will need more time on this Earth to learn to be of light-heart ...

And yet, time and his aging sisters do not place wrinkles in such places as these.

Time brings wisdom in his glass and the sisters of age come bearing gifts of a deeper compassion, a love for all life and a heartfelt kindness which is the core of an enduring, illuminating beauty ...

Anyone looking for the beauty in you that sees a wrinkle does not know Beauty ... they see only a 'wrongness', which they are comparing with a shallow, cognitive idea of a 'rightness' - and this has nothing to do with Beauty ...

If you have an adventurous, tingly desire ... coupled with a delight for the joy of life and sharing time in your sacred place .

If you have beauty in your eye when you see someone that lights your day.

If you have kindness, tolerance and acceptance for yourself in your heart.

If you have an infinite compassion for all sentient beings in your soul.

Then, to me you are wrinkle free, for you are full of Beauty ... ❤.

When light falls

Would you catch my heart while I catch my breath

Would it be my name you call

Would you be my love and delight in me

Be the starshine when light falls

Would your heart dance and laugh with me

When shadow's hand is long

Would you lay my colours at winter's bridge

Will you sing with me at Beltane's song

Would you hold my heart in soft desire

Would you love my very soul

would you be my flame until time is done

Be my sweet love when light falls

Tripping

Running through life ...

My ego tripped

And fell into a hole

When I looked up

I could see your face

Your hair was the wind

Your eyes were the stars

I could see the Earth

Spinning

     Slowly

          So very far below ...

               ... I haven't been back there since

A Day With You

A day without you

Is a day in black and white

A day without sound

A sunless day light

A day when you are here

Is not a day at all

It is a month, a year of joy

In a sweet fleeting moment

Nectar for my soul

A life with you being here

Is a life with laughter and sweet love

It is not a day in paradise on earth

It is a moment of heaven's touch

Given from above

A life with you is,

simply,

Love

Far below I can see cloud nine ...

And just to pass away the time

I thought I'd float above the grime

Above the houses, the old church hall

Above the people, playing ball

High above the great thinker's nest

Onwards and upwards, above all the rest

I have no idea how high I may climb

But from here, far below, I can see cloud nine

A thousand Stars shall bow...

The light from the nearest star
Finds here a welcome eye,
On heart-light days you drift into the dream,
Of an azure deep blue sky

But there is nothing of light that finds the Sun
As beautiful as you,
For your face, a thousand stars shall come
And bow, their honour rarely given, true

Your eyes more welcome than summer's bright day
You are the face of my deepest dreams
Sweet angel come in to my life
Come darling walk with me

Let's take the hidden paths that run
To the soft deep earth and beyond the Sun
Through shadows to the summer glade
Into the light where Soul-full love is made

Where past-times fade without a trace
My honour held in your divine grace
All of heaven's realm - all wonders of time and space
Shine in the beauty of your light;
Your face

Memory Sticks

Memory sticks...

Memory tricks....

Time slips away and discolours the view

Memory flips....

Memory hits...

Old feelings haunt the present mood

Memory fades ...

Memory betrays ...

Who said which things what to you

Memory is an ocean ...

Memory is emotion ...

Memory sticks ... and becomes you

And if my heart could craft fine words ...

If I could find words from my clumsy hands

To express how I may adore thee

Then I could describe the beauties of the spirit realm

Such, that every reader of my words would surely fly with me ...

If I could muster my craft,

The wordsmith's art,

As if by magic each notation

Were able to find its place,

Then, sweet, sweet, angel,

Every eye of this world would behold in my page

The beauty of your face

But, disdainfully, a servant poor to thee

I am,

For in my stealth,

I want to laugh and dance and celebrate my heart's joy at your affection for me,

Though I dare not call it love,

Not yet the hand of fate knows it has found its glove,

In the shadows of my heart fly bright wings of the whitest dove,

And I confess,

For it holds well my deepest soul's health,

Of your beauty I wish to drink from heaven's sweet heart,

Come, share the light of thy brightest self

A burning wish ...

Think of your most delicious sensation ...
If I am missing,
Such joy do you miss

For it is with my embrace
Paradise sings of sweet promise deep
Your fate sealed with my whispers
In your deepest heart these moments,
keep ...

I am closer to your heart than nature's wish
My flame somehow brighter
When stolen ... such bliss

I am your sweetest flame
Your most intimate touch ...
Never ... never ... never ... never ...
Can you adore me too much

Burning ... yearning ... by the gods you so wish
I am your moonlight dream
I am a kiss ...

❤

Four Arms

Four arms

Entwine in a sun bathed room

Bubbles of delight play in the shafts of golden rays ...

Two hearts

Beat in synchrony

Upon a bed of loving

For the alchemy here is stronger than even Pluto's call ...

Two souls

Blend in a unison of light

The room a chalice for their love to grow once more

In kindness, in desire, in respect, in joy, in delight in love they adore

For hours

We kiss in breathless joy

Each and every moment imprinted upon my soul

My darling, sweet angel

I love you with all the power my spirit can know

Note: on being challenged to articulate a cup of tea ...

My cup of tea

A darkened tan graces the heart of this delight

Warm and mysterious,

Secret promise of my future to be told

Strong and sensuous,

And yet fragile in my hands

All my life I have loved thee ...

Porcelain to hold

Let time bring us closer

Tell me when the time is 3

From Asia to Devon,

Fragrant and adored,

Always delightfully, lovingly poured ...

My cup of tea

If, for you, love means pain ...

Love is protective - pure love is true
Love can be hopeful - sometimes love is blue

But love can be shadowed for a life at the start
If the heart's dreadful lesson is that love's light is dark

If the arms that hold you keep you safe from all fear
Have hands that crush you - or death brings your soul tears

When love = pain
Can I take the risk of trying?
Should I take the risk of dying?
Take the risk of loving again ...

If 'love = pain', is something you learn
In the heart of your brain; your feet twist and turn

Towards love, yet away - for if love means pain
Then to find something of beauty means hurt comes again

So keep love at bay; relate with life at the side
Dip a toe, but not swim the sea's treacherous tide

But to fear love means the fear of loneliness chills the heart
A deep breath and courage may you let your healing now start

Seek warm smiles and kindness; not just in display
Find an eye with a twinkle and watch how someone behaves

Let your heart remain open; let pain pass through this time
In winter's storm spring is woken there's a new light you can find

Yes, every story has an end; Mr Death has his day
So take the deep breath and swim deep in love's ocean today

When love = pain
Can I take the risk of trying?
Should I take the risk of dying?
Take the risk of loving again ...

Heaven's waiting room

Kindness may hold my heart at the end of time

Guiding my bright and muddled mind

Another challenge to eat, and now music plays

Hades counting down the daze ...

Hands hold my heart, as soft as swans' down

Tears fall like constant rain

She cradles my memories like an Angel come to Earth

Lulling Bye now all the pain

Who can be bold enough to help a soul pass

To leave this life, dignified in serenity?

Such compassion lights the hearts in end of life care

And such a heart-light touches me

When time here is done and wisdom takes his glass

Our hearts carry such summer blooms

I would ask that she be one more light at the door

Of Heaven's waiting room

Beauty ... is

Beauty is ... a word, a sound, an expression of a feeling ...

Beauty is ... the feeling I find in my heart when I think of you ...

When I see your photo ...

When I hear your voice ...

When your kindness and gentle care touch my heart.

Beauty is ... an experience (((❤)))

My experience of you is such that I become aware of the beauty within me ...

My gentle strength ...

My desire to understand ...

My depth of care ...

The song of life I sing in the heart of my feelings ... are brighter, stronger, softer, more enduring when I encounter the beauty of you.

Beauty requires no effort, no work, no adjustment, nor distortion; beauty requires nothing, other than to be courageously free to fully express itself in the spirit of its bright vulnerability.

There is nothing more beautiful in the world than to simply be you ...

love

Dave

Just me

Why me ? ... why do you love me ?

I'm just me ... I'm just a 'me'.

There are 7 billion people in this world and at least 5 million who might be suitable for you So, why me?

My hair is like 'this' and my family are like 'that' - gravity and life have re-shaped the youth of my body and no, it's not all fat ...

I do 'that' I like 'this' I've been to these places

I forget words I want to say sometimes muttering empty spaces ...

I'm just plain old ordinary me why in the world ? ... I must be non-starter!

The others are more beautiful classy, charming smarter

I do not understand; I cannot see why you have fallen in love with just well, just me ...

You're not a just you! Oh, you're in here too? really ... really? you think you're a just me?

No way, there's no way you're just a just me - you are beautiful and wonderful by far too good for me!

How on earth can you not see ? You're amazing! ... Endearing ... those little things you do ... how could I possibly not fall in love with you!

To accept that you love me to get my head around this - I'll have to adjust how I see me and be the me that I wish ...

Is that it then? ... done? ... like a tail-feather's swish?

I go from job-lot once honey pot ... to ... the love table's best dish!

All I have to do is believe you; I am your taste, your delight, your cup of tea; that the light of your beauty finds delight in me - I'm just a drop in the ocean but you want to dive into me I'm at the heart of your world being just me.

Change brews ...

Change brews ...

In the taste of sweet tomorrow

In the bitterness of yesteryear

In the fruits of deepest sorrow

Change shoes ...

Away the blues!

Whatever path to light you use ...

Keep your smile bright in the deepest heart of you

Heart and home the earth may roam

Golden parts of ourselves we may disown

But in the weave of time's grand design

Of entropy; this harmony - our lights entwined

Can in each moment we touch the divine

From beast to Angel; we rise through the slime

Wisdom is here; clear heart - sublime

Change bruise ...

The alchemy of light in the darkest heart of living time

Change brews ...

Come love me again

Like the soft wings of a butterfly new to spring

First kisses adorn the path of future time

Like the first rays of a new born star

The light from your heart holds my gaze; the softness in your eyes like the healing tears of heaven's rain ...

Up ahead, beyond this time, my love; my soul shall once again remember thee

The shy furtive glances of our conscious mind's new meeting,

Shall rest upon the warmth of an endless flame

All the moments in silent loneliness I have missed thee; falling away now as if the golden lights at year's end

For these new seeds to your heart I now lovingly send ...

Come; let us start this new journey on love's path without end

Sweep from our history the discarded leaves of disdain

Let love heal thy pain

Come lady, come dance, come love's dream once again

Come light of my heart - set my life aflame

Come with heart-sweet kisses - let my soul sing your name

Come in kindness sweet heart, come love me again

Heart of Kindness

My soul will always love you just as my soul has always loved you,

Whether we are romantically entwined just friends; right now or past behind,

I shall love you

No matter which way the wind blows I shall love you,

Whatever lights from me touch your heart my affection will always hold the spirit of you

The multiple ways our souls relate may shift and dance in time

Over eons we converge and diverge again weaving bonds of love from light divine

Only malice or anger can cause such pain that affection then erodes as if in acid rain

Keep bright the light of kindness in your heart

Let the sirens of deep care chose the words that express your world to me ... and you ...

Bestow upon yourself permission to find new pathways to the sun and call upon Apollo's muse; the dance to light forever done - let Hermes ride the golden arc, as if over the moon to share time with you ...

In the sacred grove where Chronos and Kairos meet, happiness casts the path beneath your feet when kindness sits at the heart of all you do.

Love's Song

Like an arrow on the wind

My love flies to your heart

For every breath I breathe

Fills me with a peacefulness

Like glistening due after dark

Like a golden summer's day

In a celtic stone ring

You fill my very Soul with love's romantic joy

To touch you this night

Shadows I'd destroy

Words of love I'll wisper

For only you to hear

With white enchanting magik

I'll drive away your fears

Shadows night shall e'er slumber

Cast a'flight at this new dawn

With Thorn, Oak, and Rowan your door I'll adorn

And love's eternal spirit

Shall burn as evergreen

When your heart calls my name, and love's song we both sing

Just a moment ...

Floating over misty hills

Twilight moon still rising,

The times of autumn conscious now

Samhain fires, in the deep earth, smouldering

Lights of summer upon the river swell

Rooks return to vale and dell

Gaea dances with the Gods of light

Time falls softly to the night

Heart connections may at times be rare

Companions upon the road we share

Timeless and fragile, we are dust passing through

This lifetime of moments; made brighter with you

Love coming home

Do what you want with your life

Give yourself permission let prosperity blow wild

Open your heart and let the love in

Say, 'Yes, Yes, Yes !' to fun!!

And 'no' to anything that hurts you

Do this with each and everyone

And stop hurtful things that you do

Embrace the best in life; no more second rated glances

You're amazing - appreciate your high worth in romances

Feed your body, heart and soul with the best life has to offer

Walk past the 'it'll do' - go for gold and never copper

Be the best you, you wish to be; live out your highest values

Build your dreams with Earthen planning

Wearing soul-full gratitude shoes

Some humble pie from your life chef

Feet on the ground while starriness calls your heart to summer roam

Love yourself - love coming home

When a Thousand Blossoms Fall

When the first blossom falls

I shall remember thee

When sunlight emerges from dark summer clouds

Your spirit shall be here with me

And in times when the hand of time weighs heavy

At season's turn

My love for thee shall deepen with each moment I miss you,

For it is moments with you

For which I yearn

My heart shall learn more deeply the value of time

Each change upon the wind,

Each breath a song,

Singing in delight of you

I am bound here in time,

Touched by the light of you

Beautiful and free

When a thousand blossoms fall I shall remember thee ...

To a star I shall fall ...

And so it is
September sleeps ...

A soul's harvest as light ...
As the weight of its feet
Impressing the cosmos like feet on snow's fall

And so it is
Memory keeps
Each moment of light and shade of our hand
Like deeds written in indelible sand

And, so often it is
Fear that stands with shadow; unknown
And yet the inner eye fears what light may show
If all you have done became fully known
In the heart of your soul
A tear may fall

And yet a soul's sorrowed tear is not dark
When told ...
A light of learning is caste to hold
A troubled heart in peacefulness
Like a still breath of morning
Into life we may fall ...

And so it is
As trees discard the remnants of the Sun
The forest crowned like a sea of gold
The fruits of the year to the deep earth ... run

Scarred by life's battles ...
Thicket and thorn bring life to the thumb
For so it is
At times of hunger to panic we succumb
Lost in the maze; dappled paths we may run
We sometimes forget to play ...
in the sun
forgetting ...
our smile to the world,
is a sun ...

shine ...

The king of our forest, bringer of life
A twinkle of kindness
Eye of delight ...

It is the warmth in our heart that comforts the night
A curious mind that holds inner light
Love seems eternal, as if evergreen
And winter's long night holds a secret unseen

That turning one's eye towards the heart
Inward in winter; the alchemist path
Where one's present is the chalice
When containing the past ...

Melting sorrows in the solution of time
Transforming; by knowing and yet not expressing
Brings new forms to life
From the dust of stars, new suns burst into light
Casting out shadows
A new light shall call

And so it is
To a star I shall fall ...

Further reading

Although I have referred to a number of books and authors in the text of this book, I have not referenced it in a formal academic way. My intention has been to create an easy flow of narrative for the reader. However, I am aware that some people like to know where information has come from and also where one can look for further reading and more depth of a topic.

Not all of the following books have been referred to within this book, but I would recommend them for further exploration and study.

The Structure of Magic - Bandler & Grinder

The Making and Breaking of Affectional Bonds - Bowlby

Egyptian Religion – Budge

The Dawn of Astrology - Campion

The Web of Life – Capra

Individual Differences and Personality - Cooper

The Neuroscience of Psychotherapy (2nd edition) - Cozolino

The Neuroscience of Human relations – Cozolino

A confusion of prophets - Curry

The feeling of What Happens – Damasio

Self comes to Mind - Domasio

The Handbook of Conflict Resolution - Deutsch et al

The Great Brain Debate: Nature Or Nurture ? - Dowling

Psychology in a Social Context - Tyson, Jones, Elcock

Social Cognition - Fiske and Taylor

Nurturing the Older Brain and Mind - Greenwood and Parauraman

Affect regulation theory - Hill

The Search for the Secure Base – Holmes

Language, Consciousness, Culture – Jackendoff

Principles of Neuroscience - Kandel, Schawtz, Jessell, Siegelbaum, Hudspeth

Attachment, Evolution and the Psychology of Religion – Kirkpatrick

The Little Book Of Conflict Transformation - Lederach

The biology of belief - Lipton

The Master and his Emissary – Mc Gilchrist

Small dreams of a scorpion – Milligan

Affective Neuroscience (2nd edition) – Panksepp

The Archaeology of Mind - Panksepp & Biven

Blank Slate – Pinker

The Stuff of Thought - Pinker

The Psychobiology of Gene Expression: Neuroscience and Neurogenesis in Hypnosis and The Healing Arts – Rossi

The collected works of Milton H. Erickson - Rossi, Erickson-Klien and Rossi

The Blossoming of Olde Rowan Tree - Rowan

How we come into being - Rowan

The Twelve Houses – Sasportas

Affect Regulation and the Origins of the Self – Schore

Affect Dysregulation and the Disorders of the Self – Schore

The Mindful Brain - Siegel

Love and war in intimate relationships - Soloman and Talkin

The Actor's Brain – Spence

Social Psychology - Stanton Rogers

Consciousness: How Matter Becomes Imagination – Tononi and Edleman

Other publications by David Charles Rowan

The Blossoming of Olde Rowan Tree

An amazing work of photographic and poetic artistry David Charles Rowan MA MSc has three diagnosed autistic conditions; Asperger's Syndrome, Dyslexia and Dyspraxia and a suspected fourth, Echopraxia. The considered wisdom is that people with Asperger's are dissociated from emotion; Spock-like and dispassionate. One of the 'narrow interests', David is 'fixated' with, is understanding the human condition; its joys and passions, clarity and confusions. This entails exploring one's own vulnerability and emotional sensitivity; which lends itself to developing a sympathetic understanding of how life is for other people. David has an articulate mind and his writings on being an adult with Asperger's Syndrome has illuminated the experience of the condition for those who also live within the spectrum, enabling parents to also have a deeper understanding and clarity.

The opening poem, An Asperger's Heart, moved one parent to write; 'I have a 3 year old with Asperger's and so this touched me deeply. I can see it in his eyes how much he wants to communicate effectively and cant. your poem made me feel like I was listening to his soul speak. Thank you!!!!'

Carolyn Palmer writes in the foreword: 'There is so much here to ponder and to absorb. This is a collection of pieces taking us through life, love, longing, desire, loss, joy, wonder, beauty, in fact the whole gamut of life lived on earth, among the stars, through time, and eons of birth and rebirth. It is about being different, but also the same, in that David has plumbed the depths, desires, longings, pain, wonder and joy, that so many of us feel, though few of us are able to articulate so eloquently and with such beauty. But there is more yet again ... The photographs that accompany this wonderful collection are not only completely in tune with the words they accompany, but are works of beauty in themselves. In some ways, David's work is a love song. It is a love song, to life ...'

Available from Amazon, or, a signed copy direct from the author. Write to David Charles Rowan at this address: info@davidrowan.co.uk

How We Come Into Being

The collection of papers within this book are the complete body of work from my MSc in Psycho-Social Studies, undertaken at the University of the West of England (UWE), Bristol, between 2008 and 2010.

The dissertation thesis, Determinism and Agency in Affective Neuroscience; a Psycho-Social Perspective, is, in my opinion, the principle of my writing to date. It not only explores the neuroscience of fate and free-will, it also addresses the dilemma of nature verses nurture and resolves this with a quadrvium; a non-linear dynamical system comprising epigenetic and ontogentic potentials, cultural and socio-affective neuro-conditioning, an autobiographical past and an anticipated future trajectory, which form a synthesis of self in the present moment.

The papers from the preliminary modules of the degree paved the way for the dissertation research; setting the scene and introducing concepts which are then further explored. Although the topics of the modules were seemingly distinct and different on the surface, a unifying theme emerged as I progressed through the MSc which I found personally illuminating.

Foreword by Dr. Ania Lian - Charles Darwin University, Darwin, NT, Australia

'For those engaged in an on-going search for "outside the box" tools in order to better understand our human condition, this book, Determinism and Agency in Affective Neuroscience, offers an opportunity to engage, with the author, in a journey which explores cutting-edge discoveries in brain science in relation to age-old questions such as free will, agency and the nature of reality itself.

The book appears at a time when cross-disciplinary thinking challenges the routines of traditional research schools, pushing studies in a direction where the representatives of seemingly incommensurable fields of sciences, such as physics and biology, or, indeed, neuroscience and spirituality, frequently meet on the same symposium panels discussing and building on epistemological differences and commonalities. At the same time, progressively, mindfulness practices are being introduced to schools and workplaces throughout the Western world, with policy-makers and business executives drawing on a new body of evidence demonstrating a link between one's overall compassionate disposition and productivity.

The current concepts of well-being as a state, where individuals are given opportunities to self-actualise, relate to others while also exercising a fair degree of autonomy and control, are seen to contradict longstanding truths where these higher order emotional states were seen as secondary to more basic human needs such as the need for water, air or food. Today we know that the brain registers rejection the same way as it registers physical pain. Our thoughts and emotions are two aspects of the same process: how we feel affects the signals the brain sends to the body in order to generate an appropriate protective response. In short, how we feel influences how we think, which then impacts on our physiology and our general disposition.

The understanding that "we feel therefore we are" (Damasio & Immordino-Yang, 2009) may well summarise the extent to which our will plays a role in our fate and daily experiences. It is not uncommon that research today provides evidence for understandings which previously were seen as mere conjectures or just the product of fantasy. It is the combined imagination of scientists, philosophers and creative authors that pushes the boundaries of the universe as we know it and, in so doing, provides science with new questions. I believe that it is the purpose of the current book to engage the reader in a journey of discovery through research and questions which provoke reflection, inspire imagination and challenge the terms in which we frame the concepts of self and other.'

Available from Amazon, or, a signed copy direct from the author. Write to David Charles Rowan at this address: info@davidrowan.co.uk

About the author

David Charles Rowan MA MSc

David Charles Rowan MA MSc is an author, researcher, singer-songwriter, teacher and practitioner of both Astrology and Neuro-Holistic Therapy. He is currently undertaking a third masters degree; an MSc in Psychology and has already been accepted for a fourth, an MA in Stonehenge Archaeology.

It has been a long journey of self study and not beginning formal education until he was forty. David first read Freud when he was thirteen and is now a student member of the British Psychological Society at fifty four.

These academic achievements may be considered remarkable given that he has three diagnosed autistic conditions; Asperger's Syndrome, Dyslexia and Dyspraxia and a suspected fourth; Echopraxia.

In addition, David was not diagnosed with any Autistic Spectrum conditions until he was forty, which meant his young life, growing up as a child carer with a disabled mother. He was unable to understand himself or the world around him, finding life bewildering and often frightening. Driven by an insatiable curiosity and a need to understand life, he took his first steps into reading psychology at the age of thirteen but found it rather dry and took a Pagan path instead; studying esoteric philosophies and finding a model of human understanding in the ancient art of Astrology.

Being an undiagnosed autistic child carer was a challenge made lighter by a love of music. The 'do it yourself', philosophy of the Punk explosion in the 1970s created a cultural sense of permission and David taught himself to play guitar, spending his early twenties in bands that were fun, if not successful.

By the time he was thirty David had grasped the complexity of Astrology and how to use the map of symbols as a means to understanding the dynamics of a person's psyche. Realising he also needed a therapeutic skill, David trained in a second discipline Neuro-Holistic Therapy; a synthesis of Hypnotherapy, NLP and Psychobiology in 1993. He began teaching Astrology two years earlier in 1991, and also commenced teaching Neuro-Holistic Therapy in 1994. In 2002 he was among the first six people in the world to be awarded the Master of Arts in Cultural Astronomy and Astrology and took a second masters degree in 2008 in Psycho-Social Studies, for which he was awarded Master of Science with distinction.

David continues to practice and teach Astrology online and Neuro-Holistic Therapy, and music continues to flow from him. For a quarter of a century David has explored the human condition with students and clients and since 2008 has shared some of these insights in social media, often in the forms of poetry and photography. The short articles on love and relating David has shared for almost a decade have formed the basis of this little book of love; The Heart of Life.

www.ingramcontent.com/pod-product-compliance
Lightning Source LLC
Chambersburg PA
CBHW070137290526
45789CB00002B/524